Happy Dog Phoenix

Your Best Friend's Guide to the Valley

by Jodie Snyder

Illustrations by Jeff Jones

Printed in the United States of America

ISBN 13: 978-1-55838-205-3

2018 Printing

Text Copyright © 2012, 2018 Jodie Snyder
Illustrations Copyright © 2012, 2018 Jeff Jones

All rights reserved. This book or any portion thereof, may not be reproduced in any form, except for review purposes, without the written permission of the publisher.

Information in this book is deemed to be authentic and accurate by authors and publisher. However, they disclaim any liability incurred in connection with the use of information appearing in this book.

American Traveler Press
5738 North Central Avenue
Phoenix, AZ 85012-1316
800-521-9221

Acknowledgments

For Glenn and Georgia

And all the dogs:

Artie	*Lola*
Bogey	*Marvin*
Bogie	*Mischa*
Brando	*Mollie*
Chip	*Nana*
Clancy	*Ollie*
Dagmar	*Peaches*
Diego	*Penny*
Divot	*Pugsley*
Ella	*Riley*
Emma	*Sally*
Euro	*Sanka*
Gladys	*Simba*
Hatcher	*Simon*
Hobbes	*Tippy*
HoneyBun	*Toby*
Howie	*Zach*
Indy	*Zadie*
Kiki	*Zoey*

Contents

Acknowledgments iii
Foreword 1
Living with a Happy Dog 3
   Good Houskeeping and the Happy Dog   4
   Renting and Rover   10
   Dogs and the Car   13
   Can Dogs and Yards Get Along?   16
   Where to Take Your Dog   20
   Blessing the Beast   27
   Photographing Your Dog   29
   How Green Is Your Dog?   33
   Bringing Home a New Best Friend   36
   How to Find a Dog Trainer   39
   Basic Obedience   41
   Can I Pet Your Dog?   45
   Dogs, Lost   48
   Dogs, Found   51

Dogs in the Desert 53
   Cool Treats for Hot Dogs   54
   Keeping Safe in the Heat   57
   Can My Dog Get Sunburned?   61
   Stormy Weather   64
   Dogs and Desert Critters   67
   How to Outfox Wily Coyotes   75
   Poodles and Prickly Pears Don't Mix   78
   Winter Visitors and Their Dogs   80

Happy Dogs on the Road 83
   Flying with Fido   84
   Heading to San Diego with Your Dog   88
   Crossing the Border with Your Dog   93
   Heading Up North with Your Dog   95
   "Stay"-cations   97
   Leaving Your Dog Behind   100

The Sporting Life	103
The Wide World of Dog Sports	104
Fit Tips for Your Dog	109
Happy Trails, Rover	111
Sea Dogs	117
"Bark Parks" in Metro Phoenix	120
Dog Park Etiquette	125
Creating a Dog Park	128
Five Places to Take Your Dog	132
Dogs and Arizona	135
Digging Up Very Old Dog Bones	136
Dog Scholar: Stanley J. Olsen	139
Dogs in Early Phoenix History	141
Dick of Arizona: Mining Town Mascot	148
From Africa with Love: The Bill O'Brien Story	149
Buckey O'Neill: Hero and Dog Lover	151
State Dogs	154
Your Happy Dog's Medical Care	155
Dogs Get It Too: Valley Fever	156
When Your Pooch Is Hurt	160
Vetting Your Vet	165
Health Insurance for Your Dog	167
Doggy Drugs for Less	170
Your Dog's Sex Life	172
When Disaster Strikes	174
In Case of Fire	177
Saying Goodbye	178
Your Dog and the Law	181
Illegal Beagles and Other Dog-Law FAQs	182
Cracking Down on Vicious Dogs	188
When Fido Turns on You	190
Dogs as Heroes	193
College Dogs	194
Dogs on Duty	196
Dogs as Healers	198
How You Can Help	202
What Your New Dog Needs	206

Introduction

I love talking to people when they visit the Arizona Animal Welfare League to find a new family member. Sometimes they'll say they saw a dog on our website and they can't wait to meet him/her. Other times, they'll wander through the kennels and, when they see a cute face that appeals to them they'll ask to meet the dog, picturing the bliss of loving on that cute little fuzzy, (or big, hairy), pup for many years to come.

It's not unusual for people to choose a dog for its looks—however, we always urge them to spend some time thinking about the most important aspect of selecting a pet—their lifestyle. If they are active and love to go hiking and camping and want to take the dog along, a "couch potato" may not be the best choice. Conversely, if they are couch potatoes themselves, preferring to curl up and watch Netflix on the weekend, a rambunctious Border Collie mix might not fit in too well.

This is only the first of many decisions pet owners must make when acquiring a new dog. If they are new to dog parenthood, they will have a million questions about a variety of issues—and, as they learn their own pup's individual behaviors and traits, they'll wonder what is "normal" and what is not (hint: there is very little "normal" when it comes to our wonderful furry friends!)

That is why this book, *Happy Dog Phoenix*, is such a treasure. Not only does it answer a plethora of questions, it addresses topics that you never would have even thought of, helping you prepare for situations that might come up, especially living with a dog in the desert with its own unique challenges.

And, the fact that the author, Jodie Snyder, chose us—the Arizona Animal Welfare League—to be the beneficiary of the sales of this book is a true honor, and we are extremely grateful for the support. As the oldest and largest no-kill shelter in the Valley of the Sun, AAWL strives every day to do the best possible job of helping these wonderful and unique animals, who have suffered from abandonment, homelessness, injury and/or illness before finding their way to us.

Our job is to make them healthy and confident and then to place them in the most loving home that suits them. Making more than 4,000 of these matches each year is both rewarding and humbling. We were thrilled to make contributions to the content of this book and hope you will enjoy reading it and keeping it as an important resource as you journey through life with the most wonderful friend(s) you will ever know—your dog. And, if you need a dog to go with the book—you know where to look. Our main shelter is at 40th and Washington streets and we also have an adoption center at Chandler Fashion Center. Our website is www.aawl.org.

Happy Reading.

Judith A. Gardner
President & CEO
Arizona Animal Welfare League

Living with a Happy Dog

Good Housekeeping and the Happy Dog

Many of us believe a house is not a home unless there's a dog inside it.

But then you come "home" and see a ripped-up sofa and garbage strewn through the house and you think: this is no home, this is a mess.

But with a little planning and insight into your dog's needs, you can have a place where everyone feels at home. In Phoenix, our casual Southwest style makes it even easier to do this.

Start at the Front Door

Nothing says welcome to a clean, happy home like a thick, sturdy welcome mat. The mat is your best line of defense to suck up Dog Dirt before it gets into the house. Some people recommend wiping off your dog's paws before she comes in after a walk; at the very least, you can take your own shoes off. Speaking of mats, make sure to put an extra-large waterproof one underneath the food and water bowls as well, advises Joyce McClary of Interiors by Joyce. Water dripped on the floor can cause long-term damage to flooring and can lead to slips and falls, she says.

Mark Territories

Scottsdale interior designer Sturling Pawlik believes one of the reasons she and her springer spaniel Barkley are excellent roommates is that Barkley has free rein of the house but he still prefers his own spots. A favorite is the window seat that lets him survey the neighborhood.

Pawlik also has a bed for him in her office, and he has his own chair in the living room so he is not tempted to jump on the sofa.

"Your dog wants to please you, just let him know how," says Pawlik, who has been an interior designer for more than 25 years and a dog lover for even longer. When dogs have their own cozy spots, they are less likely to take over the entire house.

Four on the Floor

Your choice in flooring can have a big impact on how big a chore your housekeeping with a dog will be. In the Valley, tile is a popular choice, and it is a great option for you and your dog. It's easy to clean, whether it be sweeping up dust bunnies or wiping up any accidental bathroom mistakes. Another bonus: tile floors offer your dog an instant cooldown, especially in our scorching summers.

Hardwood floors are a little trickier; dogs' nails can scratch the floors. Real hardwood floors can be resanded and resurfaced. Hickory, pecan and oak will show less damage. Some engineered wood floors with thinner veneers will not stand up to those refinishing treatments as well—you may end up living with the scratches. Lighter finishes don't show scratches as easily and there are products you can buy to remove scratches.

McClary, who has been in her home for 26 years and has had five dogs, believes in the glued-down, prefinished floorings. There's a wide variety to choose from and many of them can simply be mopped with water for easy cleanup, she says.

Or check out the new tile that is shaped in planks and laid in random lengths to look like a wood floor. It has the look of wood but the benefits of tile, McClary says.

One drawback to any hard-surface floors: they can be unkind to your older dog's joints. Alternative flooring can be vinyl and new types of linoleum. Or make sure there are plenty of blankets or dog beds on the floor so your older dog always has a comfortable spot to hang out in, McClary says.

Those of us with uncarpeted floors know there is a trade-off for the easy cleanup offered by hard surfaces: we know exactly where our dogs are at all times because we hear their nails click-clicking against the floors everywhere they go. It's like a doggie GPS for your home.

It's tempting to put down rugs to muffle those sounds, but be careful. Rugs can easily get bunched up and can cause you or the dog to trip. If you are going to have rugs, at least make sure they are heavy enough to stand up to your rambunctious, hallway-racing pooch.

Window coverings is another area where some forethought can be helpful, McClary says. Floor-length drapes and other coverings need to be folded up so that Puppy doesn't pull on them or chew them. Think mini blinds, shades or shutters, she suggests. They're harder for Puppy to reach.

> *"My husband and I are either going to buy a dog or have a child. We can't decide whether to ruin our carpets or ruin our lives."* —Rita Rudner

Comedienne Rudner has it right. Carpets and dogs don't mix. Not only can dogs wear down carpets, getting the urine out of the carpet fibers is really difficult. If you are interested in carpeting, you may want to check out new stain-resistant fibers specially created for households with pets, such as Mohawk's SmartStrand.

Many more carpet manufacturers are using stain-resistant and soil-repellent finishes to make them more pet friendly, McClary says.

Choose a carpet that is tightly woven and short napped. There is a reason this type of carpet is used commercially, McClary says. It can endure a lot of wear, spills and tracked-in dirt with little maintenance.

Julia Szabo, who writes about dogs and interior design, says that rugs, carpet and other softer surfaces are magnets for dog vomit and poop. She believes dogs don't like peeing or throwing up on hard surfaces because of the potential for splash back, so they choose more absorbent areas like the shag in the living room.

Choose Wisely (When It Comes to Fabrics)

Fabricwise, Pawlik believes it has never been easier to have a dog-friendly home. There's now a wide variety of material choices, including Sunbrella fabrics, which were created to be tough enough for patio furniture but are stylish enough for your settee.

Other good fabric choices are Ultrasuede, a smooth-to-the-touch microfiber, and Crypton, which is resistant to troublesome stains, moisture, odor and bacteria. In fact, Crypton takes its pet-fabric credentials seriously, having acclaimed dog photographer William Wegman as one of its guest fabric designers.

In choosing fabrics, look for smoother surfaces that are easy to wipe off with a lint brush, Pawlik advises. Looser weaved fabrics can get easily snagged by a dog's nails. McClary suggests using simulated leather and nylon blends in dog-friendly homes but avoiding lightweight cottons, rayon blends and velvets.

Leather is an interesting choice for upholstery covering. Benefits: it is easy to wipe down and cool to the dog's touch, and a dog's natural oils can actually help condition the leather. Disadvantages: your dog will see your sofa as the Chew Toy of Her Dreams. There are several different grades of leather and the most expensive kind, top-grain leather, will handle dog's nails more easily than less expensive grades. Also think about getting a distressed leather sofa, which will provide good camouflage for scratches. Of course, you could always train the dog not to get on the sofa (good luck with that) or at least have a dog bed nearby that she can call her own.

Slipcovers, which used to be thought of as Grandma's favorite design strategy, are actually totally hip now. And that is great news for the housekeeper in all of us who wants to keep the dog and a clean home. Slipcovers can be easily laundered and switched out. Szabo suggests splurging on an extra set of slipcovers, kind of an heir-and-a-spare approach to upholstery.

Another great accessory: throws. They can help cover the chair or sofa and can be easily swapped out. Choosing throws the color of your dog's coat is also great camouflage for those stray dog hairs.

Sharing the Bedroom

Don't forget your bedroom when thinking about the right kinds of dog-friendly fabrics. There's a wide range of good-looking bed covers these days, including duvets and matisse coverlets that can be easily washed.

A word to the wise: feather pillows and puppies are a bad combination unless you want a fake snowfall in July. The puppy's nails can puncture that pillow and feathers will come out all over and they are very difficult to pick up. Go for the fiberfill cushions that can recover from abuse quickly.

It's your personal preference when it comes to having your dog sleep on the bed with you, but if you do, opt for a higher thread-count sheets. Their strength is a better match for your dog's nails. Also consider getting a thicker mattress pad to protect the bed from any mishaps.

Does your dog hog the bed? Consider extending the bed by adding a chest or upholstered seat at the foot of the bed to give you and the dog some more space to slumber. An upholstered seat can also provide your dog a stylish step stool for getting up on the higher bed, which, of course, she covets.

If you opt for having the dog sleep on a dog bed in your room, go for a coordinated approach between yours and hers. Pawlik prefers covering Barkley's bed in leftover interior design fabric so that it looks good with other items in the room and it doesn't really look like a dog bed. She also keeps a basket for his toys next to his bed. "I'm working on training him to pick up after himself," she said with a laugh, "but so far, I am the one who has gotten pretty good about putting things away."

Spic-n-Span Kitchen

If you don't like the idea of displaying dog hair for everyone to see, then shy away from dark countertops in your kitchen. The darker the countertop, the better it highlights your dog's shedding.

If you have a scent hound or any type of dog who has a nose for trouble, then you must invest in some airtight unshreddable containers for your dog food, Cheerios, brown sugar or anything else your little pooch may like to nibble on. It takes dogs only seconds to destroy paper and plastic bags while it can take you hours to clean up the mess. Also it is essential to dog-proof your garbage and recycling areas by installing baby-proof door locks from the hardware store.

Bathrooms

Pawlik has worked with clients who have had the brilliant idea of using their spare bathrooms' large walk-in showers with handheld showerheads as dog-washing stations. Just make sure the drain is equipped to handle the hair. Other clients have added dog-wash areas to their laundry rooms.

Throughout the House

Another genius idea from one of Pawlik's clients: central vacuuming, with vacuum vents stationed underneath the kitchen cabinets and other strategic areas. One little push of a lever and dog hair be gone.

Renting and Rover

It's not your imagination—there are a lot more apartments in metro Phoenix these days. More than 20,000 new units have been added over the last three years, and 20,000 are expected to be built in the next couple of years.

So, with all of that building, does that mean there is more room for your pooch?

It depends.

There are a lot of factors in finding a rental that is good for you and the dog.

Arizona landlords have the right to not rent to people with dogs, or they can limit their rentals based on dogs' sizes or breeds. They can't, however, refuse to rent to a person who has a recognized service dog.

Dog Friendly Doesn't Mean Free

Just because an apartment or condo complex proclaims itself dog friendly doesn't mean it will let Fido stay free. Landlords are allowed to charge pet deposits and pet fees of any amount.

A pet deposit is a refundable fee paid up front in addition to your regular rental deposit. A pet fee is similar, except it is not refundable.

Hefty pet deposits, in addition to rental deposits and other costs of moving, can make it financially difficult for some people to keep their animals if they have to move. Maricopa County Animal Care and Control reports that one of main reasons dogs are surrendered to the shelter is that people can't legally or financially take them to the new place.

Recognizing the seriousness of the situation, the Arizona Pet Project has focused on the issue of companion-pet homelessness—whether caused by renting or other concerns. The nonprofit can provide counseling and other resources to people facing the prospect of giving up their four-legged friends.

Making Your Dog an Ideal Rental Candidate

Arizona Pet Project offers some terrific tips on how to make your dog more agreeable to any prospective landlord:

- **Training:** The more comfortable your pet is around different kinds of people and in different situations, the better they'll behave. Consider taking a basic obedience class so your dog learns how to put her best paw forward.

- **Meet and greet:** Offer to introduce your dog to the landlord.

- **Papers, please:** Bring vet records along to show the landlord your dog is up to date on preventive veterinary care. It's more difficult to say no to a dog who is vaccinated, sterilized and licensed.

- **References available:** Bring along references for the landlord to call with regards to your pet. References could include your vet, pet sitter, or previous neighbors or landlords.

- **Photos:** Have a couple pictures ready to show your prospective landlord how great your dog is with kids and other animals.

- ❧ **Plan ahead:** Explain to the landlord about your poop-picking-up schedule and the dog's exercise schedule, reminding the landlord that a tired dog is a quiet dog. Mention if your dog is crate trained.
- ❧ **Talk up the benefits:** Talk about how your dog is a great watchdog and will help deter vandals or robbers.

Dogs and the Car

Peanut butter and jelly. Macaroni and cheese. Dogs and the car. They all are meant to be together. And sometimes you have to wonder, does the dog love me for me? Or does the dog love me because I can give him a ride in the car?

Regardless of the dog's true motives, there are some good ideas to remember when travelling with him in your vehicle:

- **Pooch as passenger:** Your dog cannot ride shotgun. Passenger seats in cars with airbags are dangerous for dogs because if the airbags deploy, they can seriously injure or kill your dog. If your car has side airbags in the back seat, place your dog in the center of the back seat.

- **No lapdogs, please:** Hard to believe, but having a squirming, panting creature at the base of the steering wheel while you are driving is not a good idea.

- **Safe in the back:** Nor can dogs roam around in the back seat. A fast stop and they will become airborne missiles.

- **Forget the joyride:** No hanging out the window. Yes, your dog loves it, but debris can fly up and hit him, or dirt and other particles can get into his eyes. If your dog really loves the open road, think about getting some "doggles," googles that protect canines eyes.

Your dog should be restrained in the vehicle. Either place your dog in his crate or restrain him using a harness that attaches to the seat belt. Make sure the crate is tied down, or it can slip and slide around the place.

Have a Car Your Dog Can Be Proud Of

You can show your support of animals with a specialty license plate that features the work of renowned Arizona animal artist Ron Burns. The plate is just $25—and $17 from the sale goes to a fund that pays for spay and neuter services for dogs and cats across Arizona. In 2015, the license-plate fund gave out more than $220,000 to animal-rescue organizations throughout the state.

You can order the plates at www.servicearizona.com (click on personalized/specialized plates) or by calling the Arizona Department of Transportation Motor Vehicles Division.

Keep a Relatively Clean Ride That You Can Be Proud Of

Ideally, in a two-car family, the dog only gets to ride in one car and the other car is kept dog-hair free. For your "dog" car, make sure you have plenty of throws or sheets to absorb much of the dirt, hair and gunk that comes with a dog.

Here's what car detailers say about what your dog leaves behind in the car: "Dog hair is one of the toughest detailing challenges we face because it often gets embedded in the piles—either end-in or grabbed by its side," says Bill Johnson of Cleaner Quicker Car

Artie goes for a drive.
Photo courtesy of Jodie Snyder

Wash and Detailing in Sedona. "End-in doesn't allow a good cross section to suck on and is virtually impossible to get out with a vacuum. Hairs that are attached by the side means the vacuum must overcome a lot of resistance, making it less effective."

Vacuuming time can quadruple if there is a lot of dog hair, he says.

Johnson recommends using pumice stones and other tools to drag out the hair little by little. "It's painstaking and slow work, stroke by stroke over the same spot many times, each time getting a little more hair loose."

The type of carpet and the type of dog hair also factor strongly into the scrubbing equation. Longer hair is somewhat easier to remove because it is less likely to get embedded by the ends.

The Most Important Thing

Never leave your dog in the car if the temperature is over 70 degrees. **Never**. The temperature inside the car can climb to 100 degrees even with the windows rolled down and the car being in the shade. Under a new Arizona law, Good Samaritans have more legal protection if they have to smash a vehicle window to rescue an animal they see in distress.

Can Dogs and Yards Get Along?

They are two of life's great pleasures, but dogs and beautiful backyards can really get on each other's nerves.

Your cheerful, tail-wagging dog can simply stomp the life out of grass, shred your plants and turn your green yard yellow and brown. Your yard can retaliate–growing plants poisonous to dogs or simply shutting down and becoming a dust bowl, threatening the health of you and your dog.

Can't we all just get along?

Yes, we can, say the Master Gardeners at the University of Arizona Cooperative Extension office—but it takes some thought and planning.

Know Everyone's Needs

First, as always, know your dog. Your dog has needs when it comes to your—or his—backyard. Is your dog a natural sentry, with an innate desire to regularly patrol his backyard? Do you have a hound, hardwired for digging out prey and leaving small craters as a result? Do you have a rambunctious Labrador who must stretch her long legs in a small backyard? And sometimes dogs' behavior isn't determined simply by breed. Past environments or poor training may lead some dogs to joyfully pee wherever they feel like it, while others potty in the same spot every time.

Then consider your own needs when it comes to the backyard and figure out how you, your dog and your backyard can live happily together.

If you have a dog who likes to patrol along your back fence, you may have to accept that this area will never be a rolling grassland. Your dog's incessant pounding of the turf compacts the soil to the point nothing is going to easily grow there. Why not put in a gravel area along the back wall?

Or you can create a distinct path by planting hardy shrubs like Texas ranger along the edge of the path that is not against the wall. In creating a rock path, think carefully about the size of gravel you select. If you have a dog who likes to dig, that gravel may be flung out into the yard.

If your dog likes to dig holes in the backyard, ask yourself why. Is he bored? Then maybe you should be thinking more about exercising the dog rather than putting in landscaping. Walking the dog around the block could easily save you some trips to the nursery.

Or you could give in and create your dog's own digging area, with soft ground or a sandpit. Hide a couple of the dog's toys in there and you may get the rest of your yard back.

Must-Haves

Your dog could be digging to create a cool retreat. If that is the case, it is a clear sign that your dog needs shade in the backyard and a way to get into the house and away from the heat.

Shade is critical for both human and hound when it comes to Arizona weather. But how do you plant and promote beautiful shade trees for you and your dog if the dog sees the tree as just one giant chewbone? The Master Gardeners have these suggestions:

- 🐾 Place protective fencing around the tree with mesh wire. Place the fencing at least a foot under the ground to keep your pooch from digging underneath the fence.
- 🐾 Spray diluted hot sauce or bitter apple spray around the tree as a deterrent.

Access to water is critical in the Phoenix area; for larger dogs, a working water fountain can be a good source of drinking water. Some dogs drink out of swimming pools loaded with heavy chemicals with no signs of distress, but if your dog is going to be outside for any amount of time, make sure she has access to clean, cool water. (And if you do have a pool, please make sure the pool chemicals are in a hard-to-reach place, away from your nosy dog.)

Here's the Scoop on the Poop

Irony of ironies, dog poop does not make good fertilizer for your yard or for the composting pile, says the Cooperative Extension staff. Your dog's poop has a high concentration of nitrogen, which browns the grass. Poop left on grass for an extended amount of time can usher diseases into your yard. When you scoop the poop, don't think of tossing it into the compost pile, either, because it has the potential to pass along diseases to humans, says the Cooperative Extension office. This is quite a bone of contention in the gardening world, with many composters arguing that it is OK to use dog waste as long as you take special precautions such as heating the compost pile past 140 degrees. The bottom line: when it comes to dog poop, be careful where you step and what you compost.

To minimize the damage to your yard from dog urine, the Master Gardeners suggest keeping your dog well hydrated. The extra water in his system will help dilute the nitrogen. Also frequent watering can help dilute the nitrogen deposited on the grass.

Tough Turfs

Being in Arizona, you may have the strong inclination to lay gravel in the front and back yarda, put in some cactus and call it a day. But you can have grass and a dog in the desert.

Think about selecting a tough turf such as Bermuda grass, says Kai Yumada, of the Cooperative Extension office. There are a couple different varieties of this turf, and if you have to plug some holes in the yard, it is important to use the same variety.

Bermuda also gives you the option of overseeding in the wintertime to keep your lawn lush year-round, which can mean fewer weeds and diseases.

The Yard Fights Back

Your yard can be harmful to your dog. Your dog will eat anything and that includes plants that are poisonous. It's a good idea to know the names of all of your plants and to know what you are planting.

The American Society for the Prevention of Cruelty to Animals (ASPCA) has an excellent website that lists plants that are poisonous to pets. Some of the names on that list well known to Phoenix-area gardeners include aloe, lantana, oleanders and sago palms.

Where to Take Your Dog

Can you make a day of it with your dog? First, it all depends on the weather. Don't even think about taking your dog out on a hot day, but if it's a beautiful cool day, then there are increasingly more places you can go with your little Fido.

And for places that do roll out the doggie welcome mat, they may have made a customer for life. A customer with a dog can be a very loyal patron.

When Connie Schorr and her family including Petey, the golden retriever, went to Moto's at 16th Street and Northern in Phoenix, the restaurant staff was extremely accommodating, moving chairs around the patio so the Schorrs could enjoy dinner and the people who didn't want to be around dogs could enjoy theirs.

If you are planning to take your dog out on the town, it's always a good idea to check on the establishments' policies. Also, bring along a leash, treats for good behavior and some poop bags just in case. (For the most up-to-date list, please check our website: www.happydogphoenix.com.)

Where to Take Your Dog

Restaurants
(Places with patios will be your best bet for canine companionship):

Cave Creek
- Big Earl's Greasy Eats: 6135 E. Cave Creek Road
- Brugo's Pizza: 7100 E. Cave Creek Road
- Bryan's Black Mountain BBQ: 6130 E. Cave Creek Road
- Heart and Soul: 4705 E. Carefree Highway

Chandler
- BLD: 1920 W. Germann Road
- Dos Gringos: 1361 N. Alma School Road
- Iguana Mack's: 1371 N. Alma School Road
- San Tan Brewery: 8 S. San Marcos Place

Fountain Hills
- Phil's Filling Station Grill: 16852 E. Parkview

Gilbert
- Arizona Wilderness Brewery: 721 N. Arizona Avenue
- Cuisine and Wine Bistro: 1422 W. Warner Road
- Joe's Farm Grill: 3000 E. Ray Road
- Joe's Real BBQ: 301 N. Gilbert Road
- Liberty Market: 230 N. Gilbert Road
- Nitro Live Ice Creamery: 884 W. Warner Road
- Postino East: 302 N. Gilbert Road

Glendale
- Cucina Tagliani: 17045 N. 59th Avenue
- Haus Murphy's: 5739 W. Glendale Avenue
- Kiss the Cook: 4915 W. Glendale Avenue
- Papa Ed's Ice Cream: 7146 N. 59th Avenue

Mesa
- Cornish Pasty Co: 1941 W. Guadalupe Road
- The Cutting Board: 2235 S. Power Road

- The Monastery: 4810 E. McKellips Road
- Uncle Bear's Grill & Tap: 9053 E. Baseline Road

Peoria
- CHAR Pizzeria Napoletana: 25101 N. Lake Pleasant Parkway
- Lakeside Bar and Grill: 9980 W. Happy Valley Road
- Peoria Artisan Brewery & Gastropub: 10144 N. Lake Pleasant Parkway #1130
- Salty Senorita: 8011 W. Paradise Lane

Phoenix
- 32 Shea: 10626 N. 32nd Street
- 5th Ave Café: 501 W. Thomas Road
- Adobe Restaurant: 2400 E. Missouri Avenue
- Angel's Trumpet: 810 N. 2nd Street
- AZ Pops: 5050 N. 7th Street
- Aunt Chilada's: 7330 N. Dreamy Draw Drive
- Cibo: 603 N. 5th Avenue
- Chestnut: 4350 E. Camelback Road
- D'Lite Healthy on the Go: various locations
- Duck and Decanter: 1651 E. Camelback Road
- Elly's Brunch and Café: 110 E. Camelback Road
- Fame Caffe: 4700 N. Central Avenue
- Fez: 105 W. Portland Street
- Giant Coffee: 1437 N. 1st Street
- Hopdoddy: 2033 E. Camelback Road
- Hula's Modern Tiki: 4700 N. Central Avenue
- Joyride Taco House: 5202 N. Central Avenue
- Kitchen 56: 3433 N. 56th Street
- La Grande Orange: 4410 N. 40th Street
- Los Dos Molinos: 1044 E. Camelback Street
- Moto: 6845 N. 16th Street
- O.H.S.O. Eatery and Nanobrewery: 4900 E. Indian School Road

Where to Take Your Dog

- **Ollie Vaughn's:** 1526 E. McDowell Road
- **Original Hamburger Works:** 2801 N. 15th Avenue
- **Oven + Vine:** 14 W. Vernon Avenue
- **Phoenix Ale Brewery Central Kitchen:** 5813 N. 7th Street
- **Phoenix Public Market Café:** 14 E. Pierce Street
- **Postino:** (two locations in Phoenix)
- **Rott n' Grapes Wine & Beer Bar:** 4750 N. Central Avenue
- **Scramble:** 9832 N. 7th Street
- **Shake Shack:** 100 E. Camelback Road
- **Short Leash Hot Dogs + Rollover Donuts:** 4221 N. 7th Avenue
- **Sip Coffee Beer Garage:** 3620 E. Indian School Road
- **Sonic** (throughout metro Phoenix)
- **Spoke and Wheel:** 8525 N. Central Avenue
- **The Farm at South Mountain:** 6106 S. 32nd Street
- **The Main Ingredient:** 2337 N. 7th Street
- **The Windsor:** 5223 N. Central Avenue
- **Tranquilo:** 401 W. Clarendon Avenue
- **True Food Kitchen:** 2502 E. Camelback Road
- **Urban Beans:** 3508 N. 7th Street
- **Wandering Tortoise:** 2417 E. Indian School Road
- **Zinburger:** 2502 E. Camelback Road

Scottsdale

- **AZ 88:** 7353 E. Scottsdale Mall
- **Barrio Queen:** 7114 E. Stetson Drive
- **Brat Haus:** 3622 N. Scottsdale Road
- **Cafe ZuZu (at the Valley Ho):** 6850 E. Main Street
- **Carlson's Creek Vineyard:** 4142 N. Marshall Way
- **Clancy's Irish Pub:** 4432 N. Miller Road
- **Daily Dose:** 4020 N. Scottsdale Road
- **Diego Pops:** 4338 N. Scottsdale Road
- **D'lish:** 2613 N. Scottsdale Road
- **Dos Gringos:** 4209 N. Craftsmen Court

- **Duke's Sports Bar:** 7607 E. McDowell Road
- **Echo Coffee:** 2902 N. 68th Street
- **Grazie:** 6952 E. Main Street
- **Hula's Modern Tiki:** 7213 E. 1st Avenue
- **JJ's Deli:** 23425 N. Scottsdale Road
- **Kelly's at Southbridge:** 7117 E. 6th Avenue
- **Lush Burger:** 18251 E. Pima Road
- **Morning Squeeze:** 4233 N. Scottsdale Road
- **New York Bagels and Bialys:** 10320 N. Scottsdale Road
- **Old Town Tavern:** 7320 E. Scottsdale Mall
- **Olive & Ivy Restaurant & Marketplace** (ask for the free doggie bone): 7135 E. Camelback Road
- **Patties:** 7220 E. 1st Avenue
- **Pinnacle Peak General Store:** 8711 E. Pinnacle Peak Road
- **PNPK Craft Sliders + Wine Bar:** 23335 N. Scottsdale Road
- **Rehab Burger Therapy:** 7210 E. 2nd Street
- **RnR Patio:** 3737 N. Scottsdale Road
- **Salty Senorita:** 3636 N. Scottsdale Road
- **Shake Shack:** 7014 E. Camelback Road
- **Sprinkles Cupcakes** (which offers doggie cupcakes made with eggs, honey and vanilla, and topped with yogurt frosting): 4501 N. Scottsdale Road
- **Terroir Wine Pub:** 7001 N. Scottsdale Road
- **Two Brothers Tap House & Brewery:** 4321 N. Scottsdale Road
- **The Herb Box:** (two Scottsdale locations)
- **Veneto Trattoria:** 6137 N. Scottsdale Road
- **W Hotel** (which is nice because they can come inside): 7277 E. Camelback Road

Tempe

- **Aloha Yogurt:** 219 E. Baseline Road
- **Casey Moore's Oyster House:** 850 S. Ash Avenue
- **Philly's Sports Bar and Grill:** 1826 N. Scottsdale Road

- 🐾 **Pier 54:** 5394 S. Lakeshore Drive
- 🐾 **Rula Bula:** 401 S. Mill Ave.
- 🐾 **Salut:** 1435 E. University Drive
- 🐾 **Spokes on Southern:** 1470 E. Southern Avenue
- 🐾 **The Handlebar:** 680 S. Mill Avenue
- 🐾 **U.S. Egg:** 131 E. Baseline Road

Stores

There are some locations such as grocery stores and larger chain stores that are not going to let your pooch accompany you. And there are a lot of urban legends out there as far as which stores will allow you. Possibly the best course of action is to play it by ear: call ahead and ask, or bring your well-behaved, leashed dog to the store and see what happens (it wouldn't hurt for you to be charming as well). Just make sure to bring along Plan B if you get the bum's rush.

Pet boutiques and stores usually welcome your best friend. For the most current list of stores that we recommend, check out our website at www.happydogphoenix.com.

Here are some establishments that will welcome (or at the very least tolerate) your dog:

- 🐾 **Ace Hardware:** (various locations)
- 🐾 **Antique Gatherings:** 3601 E. Indian School Road
- 🐾 **AutoZone:** (various locations)
- 🐾 **Biltmore Fashion Park:** (certain stores leave out water dishes) 2502 E. Camelback Road, Phoenix
- 🐾 **Bookman's:** (locations in Phoenix and Mesa)
- 🐾 **Changing Hands Bookstore:** 6428 S. McClintock Drive, Tempe
- 🐾 **Crate and Barrel:** (two locations in Scottsdale; dog must be carried)

- **EmbroidMe:** 1645 E. Camelback Road, Phoenix
- **Discount Tires:** (Valleywide locations)
- **Half Price Books:** (Valleywide locations)
- **Hi-Tech Car Care:** 2924 E. Thomas Road, Phoenix
- **Home Depot:** (Valleywide locations)
- **Macy's:** 2502 E. Camelback Road, Phoenix
- **Masterwerks Tire & Auto** (has a dog, Milo, on staff): 21824 N. 19th Avenue, Phoenix
- **Merchants Square:** 1509 N. Arizona Ave., Chandler
- **Michaels:** (various locations)
- **Noble Beast Natural Market for Pets:** 1005 E. Camelback Road, Phoenix
- **Nordstrom:** (various locations)
- **Old Navy:** (various locations)
- **Orvis:** 2011 E. Camelback Road, Phoenix
- **Pink House Boutique:** 7009 N. 58th Avenue, Glendale
- **Practical Art:** 5070 N. Central Avenue, Phoenix
- **REI:** (Phoenix and Tempe locations)
- **Staples:** (Valleywide locations)
- **Urban Outfitters:** (Valleywide locations)

Public Accommodations

- **Light rail:** Pets are allowed in carriers, but drivers are not allowed to ask for identification or papers of your "service" dog.
- **Phoenix Sky Harbor International Airport:** Dogs are allowed, if they are leashed.

Blessing the Beast

During October, many churches open their campuses for animal-blessing ceremonies to recognize St. Francis of Assisi, patron saint of animals.

Catholic and Episcopalian churches are usually where the services can be found, but sometimes innovative congregations bring the blessing to the animals and perform ceremonies at large dog-adoption events or other dog-themed activities.

Wherever it is held, the idea is that, through animals, we can all experience something more spiritual in ourselves.

Where the Dogs Are

One of the largest—if not *the* largest—ceremonies in the metro Phoenix area is at the Franciscan Renewal Center in Paradise Valley.

The center, also known as "The Casa," has been performing blessing ceremonies since 1993. It has grown to be a two-day event that draws a couple thousand people every year.

All animals are welcome, from rats to horses—as long as they are on a leash or in a kennel. The ceremony is simple, with every animal getting sprinkled with holy water and given a prayer. The ceremony is designed knowing that many of the people and animals who show up aren't church-attending regulars.

St. Mark's Episcopal Church in Mesa takes a similar practical view of providing blessings. Their ceremony is held inside a meeting room instead of the regular place of worship. It draws dozens of people who bring in their dogs, cats and birds in cages.

Some come with stuffed toys or photos of cherished companions or even photos of the wild horses who live along the Salt River.

Despite the diversity of the animals, it's a relatively scuffle-free congregation, say animal-blessing organizers. Pets seem to be on their best behavior, with dogs being the most nonchalant about the ceremony.

Photo courtesy St. Mark's Episcopal Church

Blessing Alternatives

If you aren't near a church that provides a blessing ceremony or you are just a little uncomfortable going to church, consider holding your own little private commemoration at home. Light a candle, say a prayer, give thanks or perhaps pause to think about animals that you have loved and how much they changed your life for the better.

Photographing Your Dog

Your dog can be a natural when it comes to photos and videos if you follow some simple rules. The most important rule is to make it fun for you and the dog, says veteran Phoenix photographer and dog-lover Michael Ging. Photos of Ging's dog, Euro, are Facebook favorites.

"I have this spot on my front porch that I have used as a location to photograph both of my goldens over the years," Ging says. "When the dog sees me with a camera, she automatically goes to the same spot and sits. It's just her conditioned response."

Ging gives these photography tips on how to get your dog to say cheese instead of just eating cheese.

- **Be prepared**: It's a good thing that you are almost never without your cell phone these days. Their high-quality cameras make taking and sharing photos really easy. Just make sure you get close and shoot in an area with lots of light to get the best image from the smaller sensor and lower quality lens.

- **Posed pictures**: If you want to take a posed picture of your dog outside, think carefully about the background. It shouldn't be too distracting but it should have some contrast to it. Posing a russet springer spaniel by a brick wall is not going to be your best choice.

It's also a good idea to use an area that the dog is familiar with. Going to a new site may be interesting to the dog but may overstimulate him.

Also, with posed pictures, have a good idea of what you want but don't force it. Your dog has a mind of his own and you've got to work with the "talent."

- **Avoid other distractions**: It may be a good idea to have an assistant who can hold the leash and stay out of the picture. Your assistant can also work the squeaky toy to attract the dog's attention.

When the dog does something you ask him, be sure to reward him with verbal praise. Wait until the end of the shoot to give him a treat or all your photos might be of the dog looking at your hand for the next snack.

How I Took This Photo

"One of my favorite photos of Ella is one I shot from above her using a wide-angle lens. This created a distortion that made her head look significantly bigger (as well as her precious eyes). Everyone says she looks like a cute bobblehead doll."   —Tom Boggan, Scottsdale photographer

Photo courtesy of Tom Boggan

- **Figure out the angles:** Photographing your dog at her eye level is a very neat way to document your pet. Shooting from above or below can provide fun opportunities as well.

  It's also important to get close to your subject and fill the frame. It's OK to show your pet in her environment, but you don't want your dog to be a tiny speck in the frame.

- **Correct settings:** Get to know your camera very well and become familiar with shooting in manual mode, if available. On most phones, you can hold the camera button down for a burst of shots; this really helps you to get the shot when you have the lighting, background and any props ready. You really only have a few seconds to work with.

- **Edit away:** If you use photo-editing software like Photoshop, you can crop photos for more intimate pictures of your best friend. You don't have to have the whole dog in the photo. Sometimes, the best photos are those up-close shots of just the dog's expressive face.

  There's also a good free app called Snapseed that lets you do the same things as Photoshop, like adjusting the brightness, cropping the photo and using sharpening to make the photo clearer.

- **Make friends with the camera:** Let the dog sniff the camera, and for extra anxious pets, shoot the camera's flash a couple times just to make the dog more accustomed to the sound and the light. Another good idea: have the dog relaxed before the shooting begins, perhaps taking him on a walk ahead of the session.

- **Time of day:** With all photographs, it's best to shoot in early morning, at twilight or on overcast days.

More Tips on How to "Shoot" Your Dog

🐾 **Shade**: Open shade in Arizona is a great place to photograph. Usually there's still plenty of light for your subject but without harsh shadows of direct sun.

🐾 **Light**: Speaking of light, some dogs will need more light for their features to come through in the photo. If you have a big furry Newfoundland, it's going to take extra light to see those eyes and details. If you shoot the photo with the sun behind the dog, you will get a flare on the photo, which lowers the contrast.

🐾 **Offbeat**: Sometimes the most memorable photos are the quirky ones that show your dog's personality. Tom Boggan once caught Ella licking her chops and discovered that her tongue looked monstrously long.

Euro posing for a photo. Photo courtesy of Michael Ging

🐾 **Wagging tails**: If your dog is a happy one, keep in mind that his tail could end up blurry even if his body is sharp. Shoot with a fast enough shutter speed to freeze the tail in action. Or if you want to blur it for special effect, shoot with a slightly slower shutter speed.

How Green Is Your Dog?

If the goal of recycling is to make sure we get the most out of our precious natural resources, then adopting a rescue dog seems like a really green thing to do—after all, you are saving a life.

Another green move: spaying or neutering your dog to prevent unwanted puppies.

Or, at the very least, you could use biodegradable poop bags.

You could also visit Jackass Acres K-9 Korral, one of the best-known environmentally friendly parks in the country. It is right here in Cave Creek, on the access road just east of Interstate 17 between Anthem and New River.

Nationally recognized by *Dog Fancy* magazine, Jackass Acres K-9 Korral is a typical dog park with segregated areas for large and small dogs but with a lot of ecological twists and a true Wild-West flavor.

Recycled Dog Park

There's no grass; the park has smooth gravel for the dogs. It's all natural desert landscaping. There are a few sections of artificial turf, which was donated by the National Football League. Solar energy powers its water fountains, misting systems and lights. Volunteers made the park's benches and tables from reclaimed wood. Poop stations offer biodegradable bags. Donated sculptures add to the rustic feel. Even the park's name was recycled: the property in Cave Creek has always been known as Jackass Acres.

Jackass Acres is a membership-only park, with the fees going for maintenance and upkeep. The annual fee is $35 per dog, $50 for two or more dogs.

Jackass Acres K-9 Korral is one of a kind. Photo courtesy of Jodie Snyder.

Did You Know?

Here are some more pointers on how you and your dog can help the planet:

- **Walk, don't ride:** Walk your dog in your neighborhood if possible, rather than using fossil fuels to drive to a dog park. (An added benefit: If your dog ever gets loose, your neighbors are more likely to know who her owners are.)

- **Buy smart:** Purchase/use biodegradable poop bags for your daily walks.

- **Recycle:** Old socks and other leftover household items can make great toys. Or buy eco-friendly pet toys made from organic or recycled materials.

- **Think about nutrition:** The Best Friends Dog Club of Sun City suggests buying natural pet food made from pure protein sources raised without growth hormones or antibiotics, and that doesn't contain any animal byproducts, rendered meat or chicken meals.

How Green Is Your Dog?

The city of Chandler has more traditional dog parks but has come up with an innovative way to save money and the planet.

The city had been using pre-manufactured dog-waste stations to dispense plastic mitts. The stations cost between $75 and $100, but it was the plastic mitts that made the program too expensive to expand: for 10 stations, the city spent more than $6,000 on mitts per year.

The city of Chandler came up with some innovative ways to handle the dog-poop situation. Photo courtesy of city of Chandler

Other Ideas for a Better Planet

Taking a cue from a small Northern Arizona community, Chandler decided to create their own dog-waste stations. The materials required for one of these stations—metal post, mailbox and signage—cost about $50.

The city geared up to install 100 stations; Eagle Scouts volunteered to build half of them. City employees brought in excess plastic bags from home so the parks department had thousands of bags to kick off the program. Now, 35 of Chandler's 52 parks have dog-waste stations. Just as importantly, they have a blueprint of how cooperation can create a solution that protects taxpayer dollars and the environment.

Bringing Home a New Best Friend

Arizona has made great progress in reducing the rates of homeless and euthanized pets. It's an ongoing mission, but we are blessed with many compassionate people who give their time and hearts to operate shelters and rescue groups dedicated to placing animals in loving homes.

Shelters

Shelters offer a wide variety of dogs. In the past, they have had the reputation of being depressing places where no human or dog would want to go, but many people have worked hard to turn them into pleasant places for dogs and the people who come to adopt them.

To adopt a shelter dog, be prepared to answer questions about yourself and the dog's potential new home. The shelter staff may also conduct a visit to your home.

Rescue Groups

There are number of breed-specific rescue groups in the metro Phoenix area, who frequently rescue dogs from being euthanized. The groups then assign the dog to a volunteer foster home, where he can get proper medical care, socialization with other dogs, and, most importantly, love and patience. Foster parents truly want to make sure their "foster children" end up in the right homes, so they will give you the straight scoop about a particular dog you may be interested in adopting. In exchange, they will want to know about you and the type of home you can provide this dog they have so carefully nurtured.

Your New Dog

Whether your dog comes from a shelter or rescue group, please be patient with him. He may have been abandoned, abused or surrendered by a previous family, and then he was shuffled off to a shelter, and then maybe a foster home. Your dog has been through a lot of changes, so be understanding with your new little friend.

Once he gets to your house, take it slow. If he appears to be scared, keep him in a small, quiet area to start. Don't allow children to bother him because if he is afraid, he may nip at them. Don't leave other pets or small children unsupervised with him until they are used to each other.

Allow several weeks for him to adapt to his new surroundings and up to four months to fully adjust (older dogs may take longer than young ones).

Rescued dogs may exhibit some "bad" behavior when entering a new home. Most of the time, it is short-lived as your dog gets used to his new home. If you have more concerns, call the dog's foster parents, who may have more insights into his personality.

Most animals coming from abusive homes will typically make a full emotional recovery—with proper care and attention. In fact, many people who adopt these dogs believe that their dogs know they have gotten a second chance.

What Kind of Dog Is Best for You?

Thinking about getting a dog? Here are some tips from the Arizona Animal Welfare League, Maricopa County Animal Care and Control and others to help with the decision:

- **Be honest with yourself:** How many hours are you home? Some breeds like basset hounds love people and want to be around them as much as possible. Talk with rescue groups to learn about dogs' tolerance for being alone.

- **Know the breed:** Bassets are snugglers. Chihuahuas have small bladders and need good access to a potty area. Beagles will leave no garbage can uninvestigated. Greyhounds, despite their elegant physique, are notorious couch potatoes. Don't worry—there is a dog for you.

- **Recognize the individual:** A dog's breed can give you only a very general idea of her true personality. Other factors such as how she was treated as a pup can shape her behavior as well. You really have to meet the dog to get a good sense of the animal. Ideally, you should meet the prospective dog with your entire family (other pets, too) before making a decision.

- **Do you have the right place for a dog?** Doggie door and fenced yard? Landlord OK with a dog? Not worried about your new carpet and furniture? Fence around the pool? Some breeds like bassets and greyhounds don't swim well (if at all).

- **Resources?** Is there enough money in the household budget for licensing, vaccinations, vet bills?

- **Big changes coming?** Moving soon? New baby on the way? Retiring and looking forward to traveling? Perhaps you should rethink bringing a new pet into your home.

How to Find a Dog Trainer

A well-trained dog is a companion who brings joy into your life; a not-so-well-trained dog is, well, the kind many of us have. If you want your dog to be a Canine Good Do Bee, here are some things to look for in a trainer or obedience classes:

- **Good rep?** Does your veterinarian have any good suggestions? What about friends with dogs? Rescue groups are a good source of information, and you may want to repay their recommendation with a donation to the cause.

- **Credentials?** Anyone can claim to be a dog trainer because this is an unregulated field. A "certified pet dog trainer, knowledge-assessed" (CPDT-KA) trainer is someone who has completed at least 300 hours of dog training with actual teaching time. These trainers have passed a 250-question examination. There are also national accrediting agencies for animal behaviorists, veterinary behaviorists and animal-behavior consultants. To be fair, there are terrific dog trainers who may have started their careers before there were accrediting organizations, so it may be worth it to ask them why they aren't accredited.

- **Check references or accreditations.** And ask what kind of training they have had and when they took their last refresher course. Look them up online and verify their accreditation.

- **Talk much?** A good dog trainer has to communicate with the dog and, just as importantly, communicate with you. You are just as much the student as the dog in this case. You can't reinforce what you learned in class at home if you didn't understand what the trainer was saying in class.

- **Good personality?** Do you like the trainer? Does your dog like the trainer and does the trainer like dogs? Does the trainer have dogs at home? And do you agree with the trainer's philosophy about instructing a dog? The Valley has scores of dog trainers; you can find one who will agree with you about how Fido should be instructed.

- **Realistic expectations?** Your dog is not going to turn into Spot the Wonder Dog in three easy lessons. Figure out what you want your dog to accomplish—whether it is coming on command or turning on the dishwasher—and ask what a reasonable time frame is for learning that skill.

- **Got class?** One-on-one training is great but classes give your dogs a chance to socialize. Look for classes that provide a ratio of eight to ten dogs per trainer.

Basic Obedience

There are some basic moves that all dogs should know. These commands can help protect your dog, make the dog welcome in more places and strengthen the bond between you two.

The trinity of commands is "come," "stay" and "lay down," and getting your dog to master these requires patience from you and motivation from the dog, says Brianna Kuna, who oversees the shelter-training program for the Arizona Animal Welfare League.

By beginning with easy commands such as "sit," "come" and "lay down," you can help prevent your dog from darting into traffic or dashing out the front door. "Sit" and "lay down" can help him learn not to jump on people as they enter the house. Plus, these three commands are relatively easy to learn and can help a dog learn more complex instructions or tricks.

What Is Your Dog's "Precious"?

Even the seemingly most incorrigible dog can be trained, Kuna says. It really just boils down to figuring out what motivates the dog and then rewarding him with treats, belly rubs, toys, play time, or whatever makes him happy as he makes progress, she says.

It's important to set you and the dog up for success by preparing your lesson plan before training actually begins, Kuna says.

- **Understand your dog:** Don't rush into training. It really takes a couple of months or so for a dog who is new to the house to relax enough to let his own personality come through. So use this time to figure out what type of dog is living with you (fearful, aggressive, energetic or lazy). This scouting time also provides you the chance to figure out what reward will help motivate the dog during training.

- **Just try it without the training:** If you have adopted a rescue dog, you really don't know what he has and hasn't learned. Just try a basic command and see what his reaction is. He may look at you blankly, but then again….

- **Pick your spot:** For training, you need your dog to focus on you. Pick a quiet place that the dog is familiar with to begin your session. Also, for some commands, such as "sit," it is good to work in a corner because it makes it easier for the dog to remain in that spot.

- **Pick your time:** Make sure Doggie is relaxed and happy before you start the session. You should be relaxed, too. When you're relaxed, the dog is relaxed. Also, it is important to just block out ten-minute times for training—a long, one-hour session will be frustrating for you and the dog. It's also nice if you can be consistent with the time—dogs dig consistency.

- **Start with "sit":** It is one of the first commands dogs learn. It's helpful that dogs already sit on their own, so, in this case, you just have to connect the dots between the verbal command and their natural inclination to sit.

- **Take a break:** Stop training—even if the 10 minutes isn't up—if you feel your patience disappearing. Try to end the session on a high note by reviewing something the dog has already mastered. By doing this, it will help you and the dog remain enthusiastic about the next training session.

- **No penalties:** Physical punishment such as spanking will not help your dog learn. All you need is your voice: a firm "No!" will work.

- **It's all in the voice:** Keep your voice positive and upbeat. You don't have to yell—remember, this is the dog who can hear a refrigerator door open from two miles away. Do use your dog's name to get his attention, and then tell him what you want him to do.

- **Ask for outside help:** If things aren't working, you have resources. If you adopted the dog, the shelter may have advice or support for you. The Arizona Animal Welfare League, for example, provides access to a behavioral help line for the lifetime of the animal that you adopt.

How to Get the Dog to Sit

Brianna Kuna, who supervises training of shelter dogs at Arizona Animal Welfare League, works with Clarabelle, who was available for adoption, on learning this basic move.

Photo courtesy of Arizona Animal Welfare League

1. Figure out what treat the dog loves and stock up on it. Pick a quiet time and place so the dog can concentrate on you and the treat.

2. First, while your dog is standing, hold a treat in front of her nose and raise it slowly toward the back of her head. As her head goes up, her butt goes down. Once her butt hits the floor, say "Yes!" and give her the treat.

3. Next, with a treat in one hand, apply some pressure on her collar with the other hand and say "sit" in a firm, quiet voice. Give her a treat when she sits. Repeat this step a lot.

4. Final challenge: Without touching your dog or showing her a treat, say "sit." When she does this, reward her with a treat and lots of verbal praise. If she doesn't respond correctly, go back to step 3.

5. Spend no more than 10 minutes per session trying to master this. There's always tomorrow.

Can I Pet Your Dog?

Those are some sweet words to hear, especially when they are coming from a kid. The words signal that this child has been taught to appreciate dogs and understand the importance of asking for permission to invade another's space. "Can I pet your dog?" is a sign that a child's parent is on the ball.

Children make up about half of the people treated in the United States for dog bites, according to the U.S. Centers for Disease Control and Prevention. Children also are much more likely than adults to be bitten in the face, head and neck.

To help your small child do well around dogs, teach him to offer a closed fist for the dog to sniff, and then gently stroke the dog's head and neck. Remind your child not to put his face near the dog's face or poke, squeeze or yell at the dog. Teach your child not to bother the dog when she is eating or sleeping and not to play roughly with the dog. Most importantly, your child should know not to approach a strange dog without an adult present.

It's also important for adults to be good role models for the kids in their lives by treating dogs with respect.

Dogs and Babies

It can be nerve-wracking to introduce your new (human) baby to your older (canine) baby. It's important that you prepare the dog as best you can before bringing your human baby home. Some trainers suggest playing a recording of a baby crying on low volume first, just to get her used to the sounds of when a real baby is in the house. It's great if you play the recording while your dog is doing something she enjoys, such as eating or playing. The dog will learn to associate good things with the sound of a baby. It's also a good idea, before the baby arrives, to gradually cut back on the attention you give the dog. You don't want the dog to think she is getting less attention now that the hairless baby is in residence.

When human baby comes home, praise the dog and reward her when she meets her human sibling for the first time.

As dog and baby settle in, try to give both of them love at the same time (holding baby in lap while petting the dog, for example). That way the dog continues to associate baby with a good time. Also, try to take both of them out of the house at the same time. Your dog and the baby both love consistency.

Actually, babies are easy. Toddlers, on the other hand, require even more preparation. Toddler-proofing your dog can be tough. Get your dog used to being pulled at by being liberal with treats when such infractions happen. Also, it may be a good idea to establish a "safe spot" for the dog where she can take a break from the toddler.

August the Toddler and Artie the Dog getting to know each other. Photo courtesy of Kelly Williams

For Real Dog Lovers

There are some great programs for metro Phoenix kids who love to be around animals. Organizations such as the Arizona Animal Welfare League, Arizona Humane Society and the Phoenix Zoo offer summertime programs that provide kids and teens a chance to work with animals and learn more about them.

At the Arizona Animal Welfare League, for example, kids can explore a range of topics focusing on animal care, veterinary medicine, responsible pet ownership and wildlife education. Activities include tours, crafts, games, animal encounters/interactions, guest speakers and behind-the-scenes experiences. Campers get to interact with critters other than their normal canine and feline friends: Lizards, ferrets, rats and iguanas could make an appearance in the summertime camps.

No matter what the camp, there are a lot of benefits to kids learning more about animals who are familiar and very unfamiliar to them. Campers learn how to better care for their own pets but also to think about environmental and behavioral issues and to consider science and veterinary medicine as possible careers.

Dogs, Lost

Dogs can certainly go the distance. Maricopa County Animal Care and Control has had dogs from as far away as Texas land in their shelters. How can you prevent your dog from going far and wide, and what happens if you notice he is missing?

One of the most important protections against losing your dog is to have your dog licensed. That sturdy metal dog tag issued by Maricopa County will help get your dog back home. That tag and a microchip prevent 99 percent of licensed dogs who wander away from home from spending a night in the county shelter, says Maricopa County Animal Care and Control.

Armed with the information on a tag or a chip, animal-control officers can bring the dog back to your house, open the back gate, make sure the dog is secure and leave you a note. Or the dog will be taken to a facility and you will be given a call to come pick him up.

Microchipping

Animal shelters and veterinary offices can scan stray animals for this ID device and find families' contact information. In fact, Maricopa County animal-control officers can scan a microchip from their vehicle to find a dog's home. But microchipping is not foolproof, either. Maricopa County recently participated in a study that showed microchips can migrate in a dog's body, confounding animal-control folks who routinely check only one part of a pet's body for the chip.

Others suggest tattooing your pet, with the best place for ink being on the inner thigh, as a way of providing pertinent info.

Whether you use a dog tag, tattoo or microchip, the most important rule is to keep the information up to date. Don't rely on the thoroughness of animal-control folks to track you down if you don't supply change-of-address information.

Losing Your Dog

The Arizona Humane Society has some terrific tips on what happens if you discover that your dog is gone:

- **Look high and low:** Search your house—thoroughly. Small dogs can find some strange hiding places, including boxes, closets and bookcases.

- **Canvass the area:** Walk the neighborhood with a friend or family member. Carry a written description of your pet with your phone number to leave with residents or on the door (for your safety, never leave your name or your address).

- **Let there be light:** Bring a powerful flashlight with you as you search even during the day. You may be looking in dark spaces such as garages, trash bins and crawl spaces, areas your dog may crawl into if he is injured.

- **Call out:** Did you know your pet's ears will perk up at the sound of your voice from a long distance? Just remember to stop often and listen for your dog's reply, while you are yelling his name.

- **Advertise:** Post flyers within a one-mile radius of where your dog was lost. Flyers and posters produce more results when searching for a lost pet than anything else. Use attention-getting fluorescent paper.

- **Beware of scam artists:** Offer a reward but do not specify an amount. Never send money before you have your pet back. Some scams include "Your dog is at an animal hospital. Just send me $200 to pay the bill and I'll bring him to you."
- **The nose knows:** Place strongly scented items like gym socks or favorite toys outside your home. Just like his hearing, your dog's sense of smell can help him find his way.
- **Hang in there:** Maricopa County Animal Care and Control suggests looking for at least 10 days.

Helpful Places to Check if Your Dog Is Lost:

- Arizona Humane Society: (602) 997-7585
- Maricopa County Animal Care and Control: Because of the large volume and variety of animals the county receives, they can't tell you over the phone or by email if they have your pet. Visit their centers every two days:
  - East Valley facility is located in Mesa at 2630 W. 8th Street (8th Street and the 101).
  - West Valley facility is located in Phoenix at 2500 S. 27th Avenue (27th Avenue and Lower Buckeye).
- Register your lost pet with Pets911: Pets911.com; Petfinder.com
- File a report with Missing Mutts (and Cats): (480) 898-8914
- Check out:
  - Petharbor.com
  - Straydar Facebook page
  - Nextdoor neighborhood site
  - Craigslist

Dogs, Found

Guess what?

Under Arizona law, if you keep a dog or cat and care for him for more than six straight days, you automatically become the "owner."

Congratulations!

So if you find a lost dog who you believe is your soul mate, contact Maricopa County Animal Care and Control at (602) 506-PETS (7387) to report your find. That way you have proof of how long your new Best Friend Forever has been around if the original owner ever wants him back.

If you find a stray dog who you *don't* believe is your new Best Friend, you can take him to Maricopa County's shelters in Mesa and Phoenix.

Or you can post a flyer on the county's Interactive Mapping Tool, which will allow the owners to contact you should they find you have their pet. Or you can post paper flyers throughout your neighborhood or post on social-media sites such as Nextdoor and Straydar.

If the dog has some form of identification, the Humane Society of Arizona will take him at their Sunnyslope facility at 9226 N. 13th Ave. They will try to find his owner, and they ask for a donation to cover costs.

If you can't bring the dog in, call the county and an animal-control officer may pick up the dog.

Once a stray dog comes to the county, he is held for a minimum of 72 hours as the county tries to find the owner. If the dog is not claimed, he will be sent to a rescue group or put up for adoption.

If you see a stray dog in your neighborhood and don't have him in your control, call (602) 506-PETS (7387) for county animal-control officers to come out and look for the dog.

The county picks up stray dogs in contracted cities including Buckeye, Carefree, Cave Creek, Chandler, El Mirage, Fountain Hills, Gila Bend, Glendale, Gilbert, Goodyear, Guadalupe, Litchfield Park, Paradise Valley, Phoenix, Queen Creek, Scottsdale, Tempe, Tolleson, Youngtown, and Salt River Pima/Maricopa Indian Communities. Call police if you live in other locations.

If you find an injured dog, contact the Arizona Humane Society's Animal Rescue team at (602) 997-7585.

Dogs in the Desert

Cool Treats for Hot Dogs

The phrase "dog days of summer" comes from the ancient idea that Sirius, also called the Dog Star, was in such close proximity to the sun that it was responsible for the hot weather. Plus, the Romans probably looked around and noticed their own mastiffs, Malteses and hounds were pretty much zonked out by the summer temps.

The Valley doesn't have merely the dog days of summer—we have the dog *months* from May to September (and sometimes into October), where the average highs can be above 100 degrees day-in, day-out.

Here are some special treat ideas for when the dog days hit:

- **Fun indoors:** Try out doggie day care if you are worried about your dog staying home alone during the hot summer months. Day care will keep your buddy busy and give him exercise and a chance to socialize in a safe, cool environment, says Jackie Brenda of Smelly Dog marketplace and dog wash in central Phoenix.

- **Summer school:** Nothing like learning—especially when it is done in air conditioning. Summer can be a great time for any dog to learn some new tricks with either you or a professional doing the teaching. Mastering a trick can provide a great outlet for some of the dog's pent-up energy.

- **Made for the heat:** There are special bandanas for dogs that you can soak in cool water and wrap around your dog's neck to help cool her off. Cooling harnesses and cooling vests operate on the same principle.

- **Water, water:** If your dog likes the water, Phoenix summers aren't so bad. You can set up a kiddie pool in your backyard for the dog to splash around in. Just make sure to create some shade for the pool and have some thick, water-absorbent towels at the ready. Also test the water for high temps before allowing doggie to take a dip.

- **Freeze please:** Freeze your dog's rope toys or cloth toys so he can have something cool to chew on.

- **Icee anyone?** Dr. Hillary Frank, of North Central Phoenix Animal Hospital turns salt-free fresh chicken broth into a slushee and pours it into a Kong-type toy for her dog, Ginger, a Shar-Pei–yellow Lab mix.

- **We all scream:** Ice cream may have too much sugar and fat for dogs (actually, it may have too much sugar and fat for humans as well), but there are canine varieties of ice cream and yogurt that have less sugar and less dairy in them. Central Phoenix veterinarian Nicole Young of North Kenilworth Veterinary Care gives her border collie, Sam, "Frosty Paws," and the dog loves them.

- **Other frozen treats:** You can smear peanut butter in a Kong, freeze it and let little Fido ferret out the frozen yumminess. Or, if you are feeling nutritious, frozen green beans are always good, Young says.

Sabrina's Not-Sure-Where-It-Came-From Frozen Dog Treats

10 oz. plain yogurt
4 oz. creamy peanut butter

Melt peanut butter 30-45 seconds in microwave on high. Mix thoroughly with yogurt, scoop into ice cube trays, then freeze until solid. Can be stored in zip-top bags—but there will not be leftovers.

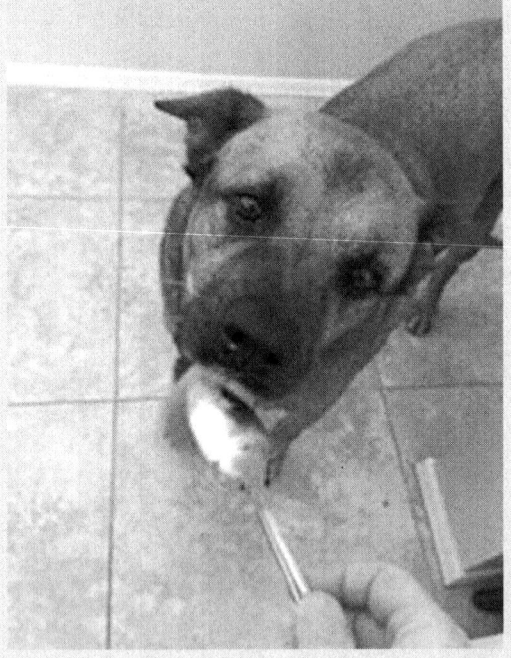

Sanka loved a cool treat. Photo courtesy of Sabrina Benton

Keeping Safe in the Heat

On one 113-degree summer day in 2017, the Arizona Humane Society emergency center treated more than 27 animals for heat-related illnesses. If you multiply that by the number of 100-degree days in metro Phoenix and the number of emergency veterinarian services, you realize how prevalent heat-related problems can be for our pets.

In fact, dogs and Arizona's summertime heat can be a deadly combination because some people can't seem to comprehend how brutal the heat can be to dogs, and dogs' desire to please sometimes overwhelms their abilities to cool themselves down.

A lot of dogs—including Maricopa County's most popular, Labradors—are happy-go-lucky souls who don't put themselves first, said Dr. Raegan Wells, a veterinarian at Phoenix Veterinary Referral and Emergency Center. "They won't tell you if they are too hot or they don't want to go out because it's too hot.

"They just want you to be happy," she says.

So it's your job to put a limit on walks and playtime, give them access to shade and water and just use common sense, especially when it's hot.

How Dogs Sweat

Humans have sweat glands all over their bodies; dogs have them only around their feet. That's why you may see moist footprints if your nervous dog is pacing the floor at the vet's office—it's her way of perspiring.

Peaches trying to beat the heat. Photo courtesy of Laura McBride

Instead of sweating, your dog cools off by panting with her mouth open. That allows the moisture on her tongue to evaporate, and the heavy breathing also allows her lungs to evaporate their moisture as well. Try this out yourself. It doesn't seem like a very efficient way to cool down.

It's even less efficient if you are a pug, bulldog, Boston terrier, boxer, Shar-Pei, Pekingese or any other short-nosed breed. Their compressed faces may be adorable but their small nostrils restrict air flow, says Dr. Kris Nelson, a Scottsdale veterinarian and author of *Coated with Fur: A Vet's Life.*

Nelson said she has seen heatstroke develop in as little as five minutes in these breeds.

Dark-colored dogs are also particularly prone to heatstroke because their dark coats absorb heat, just as dark clothes can make you hotter.

Heatstroke

A dog who is overheated will seem sluggish and perhaps confused. Dogs suffering from heat stress or heatstroke may salivate excessively, pant without stopping, show pale gums, have a rapid heartbeat, or suffer from diarrhea and vomiting. If left unattended, the dog may collapse, have a seizure, or even go into a coma.

If your dog shows any of those signs, take her temperature with a rectal thermometer. If her temperature is 104 degrees or above, get her to the vet. A dog's normal temperature is 101 to 103.

If you are at all concerned, get your dog into a cool spot, preferably into the house or air-conditioned car. If you are on the hiking trail, look for shade. Start fanning your dog and wrap her in wet clothes.

Don't put her into icy water; that can send her into shock, Wells says. Also resist the urge to let her drink too much water, she could start vomiting.

Keep Them Cool

To prevent heatstroke, keep your eye on the thermometer. Even athletic dogs can be stressed by the heat, so make sure to take walks and have playtime in the cool hours of early morning or at night.

Some people keep a spray bottle around and squirt their dogs with cool water. Others keep a wading pool of clean water so they can enjoy a quick cooldown. These are no substitutes for shade and access to cool drinking water.

Don't Do This

Even on nice days, your car can become an oven. When it's 85 degrees outside it can get up to 102 in 10 minutes in your parked car with the windows rolled up. After 30 minutes, it will be 120 degrees in that automotive oven.

Even with the windows cracked, it can still get blistering hot in there **and it is no place for a dog.**

Under state law, it is considered animal cruelty for a pet owner not to provide adequate shelter, water and medical attention. It is also illegal to leave a pet in a vehicle when injury or death could occur. In most cases, animal cruelty is a Class 1 misdemeanor, punishable by up to six months in jail and $2,500 in fines.

If you see a dog locked in a car, according to Maricopa County Animal Care and Control, call 911.

Hot in the City

Sizzling sidewalks are another summer hazard. Dog experts are fond of saying if a surface is too hot for your hand, then it's too hot for a dog's paw. Dogs' paws can blister and crack if they are exposed to superheated surfaces.

Consider using booties to protect your dog's tender pads or, better yet, ask yourself: Is it really necessary for my dog to be out in the heat?

It's not just sidewalks that have the sizzle. A pickup truck bed can seriously burn a dog's feet and give off additional heat, making it easier for her to get heatstroke. Put her in the cab instead.

Heat Exhaustion

Heat exhaustion in dogs can lead to serious and potentially fatal conditions such as heatstroke and cardiac arrest. Early warning signs of heat exhaustion can include:

- Being less responsive
- Glazed eyes
- Excessive drooling
- A rapid heart rate
- Dizziness or lack of coordination
- Aggressive panting
- Diarrhea
- Vomiting

Can My Dog Get Sunburned?

Yes, it is so bright in Phoenix that you have to wear shades, but does that mean your dog has to as well?

Not exactly, but just as you have to take precautions against the ever-shining Phoenix sun, you need to look out for your dog as well.

Skin Cancer and Dogs

You may think that your dog's fur coating protects him against the sun—but not necessarily. Skin tumors, which may be cancerous, are the most common tumors found in dogs, says Dr. Hillary Frank, veterinarian and owner of North Central Animal Hospital in Phoenix.

Not all tumors are cancerous. About a third of all tumors in dogs directly relate to some form of skin cancer. Some types of skin cancers, including melanomas and mast cell tumors, are fatal if untreated, says Frank.

Most skin cancers appear as a lump on or just below the skin or as a sore that just doesn't heal. Pets with skin cancer often show no obvious symptoms but may experience discomfort or itchiness on that spot. If you find any kind of suspicious lump, get your dog to the vet ASAP because when caught early, many cases of pet skin cancer can be treated successfully.

Dogs between the ages of six and fourteen are most susceptible to skin cancer, but it can occur at any age.

To Shave or Not to Shave?

Many well-meaning people get their dogs shaved at the beginning of the summer, thinking it will keep them cool. However, veterinarians say it is better to holster the clippers. Shorter-haired breeds don't benefit from being shaved; it only increases their risk of sunburn. Other breeds such as retrievers and herders have a double coat of short and long hairs that help insulate them from the heat. Think of the double coat as your dog's attic insulation. With it, it is easier for her to maintain a comfortable temperature throughout summer.

Black dogs are at greater risk for malignant melanomas on the toe or in the toenail bed. Specific breeds are at risk for mast cell tumors: boxers, as well as Boston terriers, Labrador retrievers, beagles and schnauzers.

The Coat Can Make a Difference

Coat color can make a difference when it comes to your dog's ability to fight off the damaging effect of the sun's ultraviolet rays.

Lighter-colored animals are much more prone to sunburn and skin cancer than those with darker coats.

All dogs have certain areas, such as the nose and the pads of the feet, where there is nothing to shield sensitive skin from the sun.

Sunblock Precautions

Just like you and me, some dogs love to sunbathe, feeling a few rays on their tummies.

The American Kennel Club recommends limiting your dog's exposure during the day and applying sunblock to his ears and nose 30 minutes before going outside.

Be careful with the sunblock. Chances are your dog is pretty good at licking it off. Swallowing the cream may be worse for your pooch than her getting an actual sunburn. Try to apply it to her head, neck and back.

Some people put white-colored T-shirts on their dogs to act as a sun barrier, said Dr. Raegan Wells, a veterinarian who specializes in emergencies. She is on staff at Phoenix Veterinary Referral and Emergency.

If your dog does manage to get a sunburn, cool her off with a mist from a water bottle or apply some cool washcloths to the affected area and keep a watch over it for possible infection.

Frank recommends that people give their pets a quick check every month for any new lumps that could be signs of tumors. She suggests working slowly around your dog's body, moving the fur and looking at the skin. Make this a regular routine while brushing and you may catch skin cancer at its earliest stages. And as with most things, an extra treat at the end of the checkup will make it go even easier.

Stormy Weather

Summer monsoons in Phoenix are when Mother Nature shows us who's boss. Buckets of rain. Dust storms. Pyrotechnic lightning displays. Thunder. Winds that shake the house.

Your dog, however, may not be impressed—he may just be terrified.

The Phoenix monsoon season, which generally starts in July, is one of the busiest times of the year at the Maricopa County Animal Care and Control shelters. Dogs frightened by the loud booms of thunder and electric cracks of light make a run for it to get away from the horrendous noise. And frequently, fences get blown over, which makes their escape even easier. It's a one-two punch that makes animal shelters overcrowded with dogs who just wanted to run away from the storm and ended up running away from home.

Keep Your Dog Safe

Make sure your dog has secure, up-to-date and easy-to-read identification at the beginning of the storm season, say Maricopa County Animal Care and Control staff. (Other busy times for the shelters are Fourth of July and New Year's Eve).

A dog's reaction to storms has more to do with her training, environment and past experiences than the type of breed she is, says Dr. Stephanie Young, a veterinarian with North Kenilworth Veterinary Care in Phoenix. No matter the breed, as dogs get older, they may develop storm anxiety. University of Pennsylvania researchers believe about 15 to 30 percent of dogs can experience "thunderstorm anxiety."

Many dogs can sense when a storm is coming, perhaps because they can detect a drop in barometric pressure. Or they can pick up smells of a coming storm with their uber-sensitive noses or hear far-off vibrations with their keen hearing.

As the monsoon gets closer, some dogs start to pant excessively and become restless. Others take more dramatic action: breaking down doors or jumping through glass windows.

Shelter from the Storm

There are a number of suggestions for how to help your dog through the monsoons, including designating a secluded area such as a closet where he can go to feel safe. Crating may be too dangerous, as he could become overly agitated and hurt himself in the crate while trying to escape the storm. Giving treats and doing things the dog loves (fetching, getting belly rubs) may help soothe him.

Or you can use ThunderShirts, cloth wraps that apply pressure evenly around a dog's torso. Many people swear by them, but scientific findings are mixed. It is important to make sure your dog doesn't overheat from wearing them, especially during summer storms.

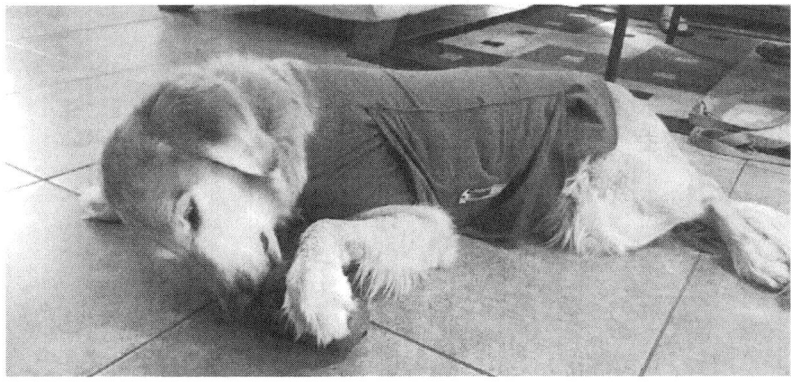

Kal, wearing his ThunderShirt and being distracted by a frozen Kong filled with peanut butter. Photo courtesy of John Phoenix

Other items you can try include diffusers, sprays or collars that send out dog-appeasing pheromones similar to the pheromone secreted by nursing dogs. Again, reports of success with these are anecdotal.

Many vets prescribe anti-anxiety medications, which can vary in length of time to take effect. Some dogs develop balance problems after taking these drugs and they need to be watched around stairs.

No matter what option you consider, it's important to remember that the dogs' reactions to thunderstorms and lightning are involuntary. Punishing and yelling at dogs won't calm them, say University of Pennsylvania researchers. So, the storm and all of its theatrics may provide you a reason to hunker down with your best friend and remember how much you love him, anxiety and all.

Dogs and Desert Critters

The desert around the Valley is one of the most unique natural environments in the world. We're on the upper edge of the Sonoran desert, one of the hottest—and driest—of all the deserts. Our rainfall patterns are unusual, our geology is stunning and our weather can be out-of-this-world hot.

So chances are that your dog, inquiring creature that he is, will encounter his fair share of unique desert dwellers: deadly spiders, wild-hog-looking creatures, giant mutant-like lizards and deceptively dangerous toads. It's not just the dogs who hike Arizona trails that will encounter these critters; increasingly, dogs who live in homes near the desert are getting up close and personal with them.

Deadly Spiders

In the Phoenix area, two types of spiders to be especially careful of are the Arizona brown spider and the black widow, says Malinda Malone, who teaches pet first-aid classes for certification.

The Arizona brown spider is small and inconspicuous, with darker brown markings that vaguely resemble the shape of a violin on its head and abdomen. It's an arachnid cousin of the brown recluse spider found in the Midwest. Black widow spiders are black and shiny; the venomous female has a reddish hourglass shape on the underside of her abdomen.

Also be aware of tarantulas, big hairy spiders that can be up to four inches in size. Although they look ferocious, tarantulas usually keep to themselves and their venom isn't too potent. But if your dog does tangle with a tarantula, it is best to get him to the vet anyway. As with bee stings, reactions to tarantula bites can run the gamut.

If your dog gets bitten by a spider, he may not notice it. Nonetheless, if you suspect your dog has been bitten by a spider, contact your veterinarian immediately. They may recommend administering Benadryl or an ice pack to prevent inflammation. Most likely they will have you bring the dog in so they can determine the severity of the bite and treat the symptoms.

Rattlesnakes and Dogs

Arizona is number one among U.S. states in having different types of rattlesnakes, including the western diamondback, which has the dubious distinction of being responsible for more bites in humans than any other U.S. rattlesnake.

Because of their size, dogs are more at risk of dying from a snakebite than humans. Also, dogs tend to investigate critters with their noses and are most likely to get bitten on the head and face, close to major arteries. Venom can also cause swelling in the dog's face, making it harder for them to breathe. At the same time, venom can affect the liver, kidneys and even the heart.

Many people who live in the metro Phoenix area believe that their dogs need to go through snake-avoidance training; others are flat-out leery of the programs, which rely mostly on punitive punishment, including electric shock collars.

It's a difficult decision to make: use potentially brutal training tactics or face the risk of your dog being killed by a snake. In deciding, consider your dog's age, weight and temperament as well as your proximity to snakes. If your dog is shy, aggressive or gets upset after a challenging experience, then she is not a good candidate for this type of training. If you decide in favor of the training, please check out the trainer and his or her references thoroughly.

There is a vaccine available for dogs that can decrease the severity of a rattlesnake bite. The vaccination requires booster shots, and it doesn't eliminate the need for medical treatment if your dog has been bitten. Nor does it provide protection if your dog is bitten by a different type of snake.

Some other things you can do to protect your dog from snake encounters include:

- **Avoid "snakey" areas:** Keep an eye out for warnings at trailheads about snakes; also, news coverage usually mentions where people are being bitten.

- **Keep your dog on a leash:** Having your dog closer means you can manage her better if you do encounter a snake. If she is kept on the trail, that will help her avoid tall grass and rock piles where snakes like to reside.

- **Avoid "snakey" times:** The warmer the weather, the more likely that the snakes will be out. Snake season usually begins in March and ends in October; during the summer, they are most active at night.

- **Know before you go:** Have the phone number of the nearest animal-emergency center on your speed dial. You want to be prepared if you think your dog has just been bitten. Local vets may not have antivenin in stock but emergency centers should have some in reserve.

- **Avoid snakes and coyotes at the same time:** If you live in desert areas, employ the same commonsense ideas that you use to avoid coyotes in the backyard: remove food sources such as quail blocks and dog food left outside.

Stinging Scorpions

Arizona has more than 50 species of scorpions, but only one, the bark scorpion, has a sting that can cause medical problems. Unfortunately, it is the most common one found in people's homes. If you live in a bark scorpion's territory, you will most likely have them inside your house.

The bark scorpion has slender pincers, a tooth at the base of its stinger and a long triangular sternum.

If you notice your dog move suddenly, act startled or jump for no apparent reason, consider that he may have been stung by a scorpion, says Malone.

Call your vet quickly, because the tinier the dog, the stronger effect the scorpion's venom can have, she says. The vet can remove the scorpion stinger and clean the wound.

Wild Pig-Looking Creatures (Javelina)

Javelina look like pigs but are actually members of the peccary family, a group of hoofed mammals originally from South America. That distinction won't matter when you encounter one, because either its looks or its smell will catch you off guard. Weighing in at 40 to 60 pounds, sporting some ferocious teeth and usually traveling in herds, javelina should get your respect. Stay out of their way.

Javelina aren't looking for trouble, but they have been known to take on dogs as big as Labradors if they feel cornered or to protect their young. The Arizona Game and Fish Department warns that dogs are natural predators of javelina, and the two can seriously hurt or kill each other. If you see a javelina while walking your dog, avoid going near it and quickly take your dog in a different direction.

If your dog does get tangled up in a fight, do not wade into the middle. Getting mauled yourself doesn't help your dog. Stay to the side and try to break up the fight as best you can, using air horns, water, pepper spray or anything else that may be handy.

Rapacious Raptors

Even the birds in Arizona can be dangerous to dogs. Arizona has raptors, such as falcons, eagles, hawks and great horned owls, flying around our sometimes unfriendly skies. And these birds have been known to swoop down to take off with small dogs (those who weigh 20 pounds or less).

The birds can be especially threatening during nesting season when they are trying to protect and feed their young. Your Yorkie may be just the right size for a hawk and his family to dine on.

To keep your dog safe, keep an eye out for any large birds in the areas, in your backyard or along your walking path. If you see one in your yard, bring your dog inside and, from a safe distance, try to scare off the bird with loud noises, whistling, even banging pots and pans together.

If you've noticed that a raptor seems to have built a nest in your yard, be sure to keep your dog away until the baby birds have left the nest—that will keep the dog and babies both safe.

Giant Mutant-Like Lizards (Gila Monsters)

Gila monsters: Stout, slow-moving and clothed with shiny, beaded exteriors, they are the largest lizard native to Arizona and the only native venomous lizard in the United States.

Despite its Hell's Angel–like exterior, it's the Gila monster that is often the prey. In fact, it is the first venomous animal in North America to be legally protected.

Domestic cats and dogs often kill Gila monsters, so chances are your Fido may not back off from a tussle with one of them. It's the Gila monster's bite that can be more dangerous than its venom; these lizards will bite a predator and hold on for dear life. If a Gila monster does grab your dog, use a prying instrument to open the lizard's jaws. To perform immediate first aid, flush and soak the wound, and if there are any remnants of the lizard's teeth, remove them. Get your dog to the vet, where they can prescribe antibiotics and painkillers and check the dog's heartbeat to make sure the venom is not causing arrhythmia.

Deceptively Dangerous Toads

It's not the same as kissing a frog, but some dogs can't help themselves—they lick toads. There's real trouble when they lick the Sonoran Desert toad (also known as the Colorado River toad). These toads come out during monsoon season to feed and breed, frequenting rain puddles or swimming pools.

They look like your basic toad: plump, in camouflage colors of green or brown. But these toads can squirt out a milky white toxin to dissuade anything from messing with them.

Signs of when your dog has licked the wrong toad include foaming at the mouth, drooling, seizure and a fast heartbeat.

Seizures and death can occur in dogs within 30 minutes from licking a Sonoran Desert toad. Get your dog to the vet as soon as you can, but if you observe your dog with one of these toads, perform immediate first aid just in case:

1. Turn on the garden hose and rinse out the front of your dog's mouth. Don't force water down the back of the dog's mouth or he may choke. Depending on your dog's exposure, continue rinsing his mouth for up to 10 to 15 minutes.

2. Rub the dog's gums and wipe off his nose to help remove any toxic slime.

Vets say that most dogs never learn from a toad poisoning, so it is important to keep your dog inside after dark and supervise him when he is outdoors.

Critter-Proofing

There are many simple things you can do around your house to keep the creepy-crawlies out and your canine friends safe. Here are some tips from the University of Arizona Cooperative Extension office:

* Don't rely just on pesticide treatments done by pest management professionals or one-time sprays that you do yourself.

* Screen all doors or windows that can be opened and all ventilation openings. Keep the screens in good shape.

* Install door sweeps or thresholds on all exterior doors. You should not see light coming from underneath the door.

* Fill small cracks around windows, doors and in fascia boards with high-quality silicone or acrylic latex caulk.

* Remove loose boards, woodpiles, rocks and debris from areas around your home.

* Don't store your shoes outside overnight if you are worried about scorpions.

* If scorpions have been found in your area, conduct a nighttime reconnaissance using a battery-operated camp light equipped with a black (UV) fluorescent bulb. Scorpions glow brightly under black light and can be seen up to several yards away.

* If you are concerned about spiders, clean your house thoroughly, particularly closets, basements and behind outside shutters. Dust regularly along doors, windows, vents and foundations.

- ❧ Reduce clutter in storage cupboards; don't place your hands where you can't see what you are picking up.
- ❧ Vacuum up webs, unwanted spiders and egg sacs.
- ❧ Install yellow or sodium vapor light bulbs outside your doors. They attract fewer insects, thereby drawing fewer spiders to the area.
- ❧ Don't collect wood from outdoor woodpiles without wearing gloves. Place wood from outside directly on fires. Don't store wood indoors.

How to Outfox Wily Coyotes

Although they are animal-kingdom "cousins," coyotes and dogs don't really mix. In fact, coyotes pose a great danger for small and toy-sized dogs.

A coyote looks a lot like a thin German shepherd with a bushy tail. Coyotes usually weigh in at 22 to 42 pounds.

They normally live in the desert but have been known to hang out in decidedly urban parts of the Phoenix area such as Central Avenue and Indian School Road.

It is not a good feeling when you see a coyote and all you are armed with is a hot-pink retractable leash and a roll of biodegradable poop bags. Neither item is a good deterrent against a predator like the coyote.

Seeing a Coyote While Walking Your Dog

Experts say the coyote is not going to bother you if you are out walking your dog (but then again, they are not out there with you, the pink leash and the poop bags). If you are walking the dog and see a coyote, move on.

Don't turn away or run, because the coyote may see it as an opportunity to chase you. Keep eye contact as you move toward other people, a building or an area of activity.

You can make eye contact, yell and make noise, wave your hands over your head and do your best to look as big and as intimidating as possible.

If coyotes live in your neighborhood, keep your dog on the leash during your walks. Don't let your dog chase, bark at or attempt to play with a coyote under any circumstances. Coyotes may look like scrawny dogs but they are surprisingly strong and can travel in packs.

If you are walking your dog in an area known to have coyotes, it may be a good idea to carry a walking stick, air horn or whistle. Some people carry "coyote shakers," aluminum cans filled with coins.

Owners of large and medium-sized dogs have little to worry about. Coyotes know they are overmatched by large dogs and will usually back off.

But smaller dogs are a different story. Very small dogs, such as small poodles, are viewed by coyotes as easy prey and are at risk of being killed year-round. Coyotes have been known to jump fences to get at a small dog.

Conflicts between dogs and coyotes occur primarily in the months of March and April, says the Arizona Game and Fish Department. It's the time of the year when coyotes are setting up their areas for the soon-to-arrive pups and they become exceptionally territorial. If you are too hospitable toward them, they will consider your backyard to be their territory and have been known to attack dogs as large and powerful as Rottweilers to protect their space.

Remove the Welcome Mat

The Arizona Game and Fish Department says that coyotes are in your neighborhood because they have sized it up as a good place for food, water or shelter. How does your home stack up?

- **Food:** Food can include unattended pets, birds or rodents attracted to bird feeders, pet food, garbage or fallen fruit.
- **Water:** Water sources can include a pet's water bowl or a swimming pool.
- **Shelter:** Shelter can include a storm drain or any cave-like area beneath a shed or unused building.

If you are providing any of these items, it may be time to stop being such a gracious host:

- **No more free lunches:** Don't feed coyotes—and that includes leaving dog food outside.
- **No more free lodging:** Block off possible sites for dens with fencing or other devices.
- **No more "friends":** Keep small household pets indoors.
- **Be obnoxious:** Shout at the animal, bang pots and pans together or spray the coyote with a hose from a distance.
- **Be bright:** Keep your area well-lit at night.
- **De-fence:** A fence at least six feet high will be a deterrent. Be sure the fence is buried at least one foot into the ground (with an apron base) so coyotes will not be able to dig under it.

Poodles and Prickly Pears Don't Mix

That Arizona icon, cactus, can be a sticky and painful problem for your dog. If you have cactus around your home, make sure your dog doesn't have easy access to it. If you are heading out to the Great Outdoors, it's a good idea to know the area and avoid the cactus patches. And be patient as your dog learns the hard way (repeatedly) about cactus.

It's also a good idea to be prepared. Many hikers and hunters carry a pair of hemostats (those devices that look like a cross between scissors and needle-nose pliers) and a coarse-toothed comb to help remove cacti from canines.

The curved type of hemostats can reach a lot of angles when used to pull out cactus needles that become imbedded in a dog's feet.

A comb can be used to literally comb out the needles—pull it through the cactus and they should come out. Follow up with the hemostats on any individual needles that may be left. Here are some other suggestions for dealing with a "stuck" dog:

- **In the eye:** If a cactus needle becomes imbedded in a dog's eye or other vital area, leave it to the vet. The vets can put dogs under anesthesia, making it less painful for everyone (yourself included) for the needles to be removed.
- **Be thorough:** Grab a flashlight so you can look at the area to make sure you get all the needles out. Removing cactus from a dog can be a two-person job.

- **Use the right tools:** Use a clean pair of hemostats or needle-nose pliers to remove the needles.

- **Got teeth?** Many times, dogs will try to bite at the cactus to remove it. While this is sometimes effective, it may mean you have to go into the dog's mouth to remove cactus that get stuck in there. Consider going to the vet in this case.

- **Keep a careful watch:** Depending on how many needles got stuck in the area, let nature take its course or use some antibiotics. Be on the lookout for any signs of infection.

Foxtails

Other pointy objects that dogs should avoid in the field are foxtails, dried seed heads of western grasses. When the winter grasses turn brown in the spring and summer, the seed heads break off easily. These foxtails are pointed on one end and spiked on the other, much like a fishhook. Foxtails can break off and burrow themselves beneath eyelids, down ear canals and between toes and work their way into the brain, spinal cord and lungs.

If your dog starts rubbing her eyes, shaking her head and digging at her feet, take her to the vet to be checked out. The vet is your best bet to remove these stubborn pests.

The best way to treat foxtails is to prevent them. Keep your lawn mowed. Stick to trails and avoid foxtail-infested areas. Thoroughly brush and inspect your dog's coat if she has been romping through tall, mature grass. Keep your dog groomed and check your dog's ears and feet regularly.

Winter Visitors and Their Dogs

Every fall, the Valley witnesses the arrival of winter visitors. Not only do our "snowbirds" bring along their shorts and bottles of sunscreen, they also come with their canine companions. Here are six things winter visitors should know about staying here with their dogs:

- **Dog parks galore:** Unlike Back Home, there are plenty of dog parks in the metro Phoenix area. It's a good idea to explore them all, and the winter weather is certainly the right time for it.

- **Welcome mat at many trails:** Leashed dogs are allowed at most municipal hiking trails (cities of Phoenix, Glendale, Scottsdale and others). Arizona's state parks have a little more regulation: leashed pets are welcome at most but not allowed at Red Rock State Park or on the trails at Tonto Natural Bridge State Park. National parks in Arizona vary in how dog friendly they are. At Saguaro National Park, dogs aren't allowed on unpaved trails; at Painted Desert, there are special activities for them, complete with dog treats. And the biggie, the Grand Canyon, allows leashed dogs on the trails above the South Rim but not down into the canyon. Options for dog-friendly areas are even fewer at the North Rim. If you are planning to visit national parks and monuments, it really pays to check ahead

- **Classes and groups:** There's also a really good supply of classes and groups who welcome people who are staying just for the season. The list of activities runs the gamut from dogs jumping off docks to dogs dancing with their human partners in canine freestyle, says Sharon Howarth, a professional dog trainer and owner of Back to Basics.

- **Enjoy the weather:** Your dog is going to love the weather just as much as you do. Just don't overdo it—allow your dog to get acclimated to having plenty of sunshine. Even though it's wintertime, bring along the water.

- **Get out and about:** Many restaurants in the Valley allow well-behaved dogs. The Best Friends Dog Club of Sun City is one source of neighborhood places you may want to check out.

- **The season is right:** Only staying for a couple of months? Many hospitals and other nonprofits are glad to work with seasonal volunteers. Look for opportunities where you and your dog can help out near you.

Did You Know?

Your dog can pick up Valley Fever easily in metro Phoenix but your vet Back Home may be unfamiliar with it. If your dog has symptoms such as low energy, lack of appetite, coughing or limping, have him checked out.

Test Yourself

How well do you know about dogs and the desert? Why not take our little quiz to find out for yourself? (You can always ask the pooch for help if you get stuck.) Pick the best answer:

1. How do dogs sweat?
    a. Through their fur
    b. By breathing
    c. Through the pads on their paws
    d. They're too cool to sweat
2. What's the best way to prepare your dog for summer?
    a. Book her a flight to San Diego
    b. Shave her
    c. Check her for any signs of skin cancer
    d. Bump down the AC in your house a few degrees
3. What should you do if you and the dog see a coyote?
    a. Go over and make friends
    b. Run away
    c. Make a lot of noise and wave your arms
    d. Do nothing
4. What is **not** an option when it comes to keeping your dog calm during monsoons?
    a. Put him in a ThunderShirt
    b. Crate him
    c. Distract him with goodies
    d. Have him wear a collars with pheromones
5. Your dog got into some cacti. What should you **not** do?
    a. Use a flashlight to make sure you get everything
    b. Let the dog get it out with her teeth
    c. Go the vet if there are signs of infection
    d. Use a comb, tweezers or hemostats to get the needle out

Answers: 1-c; 2-c; 3-c; 4-b; 5-b

Happy Dogs on the Road

Flying with Fido

Dogs: you can't FedEx them.

So if you are going cross-country and you want to take Spot with you, it's likely your journey will include either the car or the airplane.

First, really think about if you need, absolutely need, to take your dog with you on a flight. The Humane Society of the United States recommends that you do not transport your pet by air unless absolutely necessary. If you must transport your pet by air, your best option is to take your pet in the aircraft cabin with you, according to the society. As long as your pet is a cat or small dog, some airlines will allow you to take the animal on board for an additional fee.

Booking a flight for your dog can be complicated. Increasingly, fewer airlines will accommodate dogs in the cargo area underneath the plane because of the dangers of potentially overheated and icy-cold areas for dogs, especially short-nosed breeds.

One of the busiest carriers flying out of Phoenix Sky Harbor International Airport—Southwest Airlines—will only take dogs in the cabin section. The dog must fit in a carrier that can be stowed under a seat. You can expect to pay a set passenger fee each way for your dog's flight.

Read the Fine Print

Airlines' policies toward dogs as passengers vary as much as their guidelines for extra bags. It's important to do your homework and understand your carrier's policy before booking a flight. And policies can change literally in an instant.

When making your reservations, go ahead and reserve a spot for your dog, as pet reservations are first come, first served; airlines have different limits on how many pets they will allow on a plane. Some won't accept certain breeds on the plane at all. Try to book a nonstop flight and avoid traveling during the hottest and coldest parts of the day.

The Carrier

If you are planning to take your dog on a flight, you need a soft- or hard-sided pet carrier that is leakproof and well ventilated to carry him in. It must be small enough to fit under the seat in front of you. Select one that allows your dog to stand up and turn around in the carrier with ease.

In the Cargo Hold

Some carriers still offer to put Fido in cargo, but federal regulations prohibit live animals flying as excess baggage or cargo if they will be exposed to temperatures that are below 45°F or above 85°F for more than four hours during departure, arrival or while making connections.

Getting Your Dog Ready to Fly

No matter whether your dog is in first class or cargo, check with your veterinarian to make sure your dog should even be on board. Federal regulations require your dog to be at least eight weeks old and weaned. Ask your veterinarian if it would be best for your dog to be tranquilized for the trip and what kind of feeding schedule he should be on.

Expect to provide a certificate of health as well as rabies and vaccination certificates to the airlines.

Make sure to pack a blankie for your dog. It gets chilly on flights and it's always nice to have something with the reassuring smells of home. Be careful, however, that the blanket isn't so thick that it interferes with the dog's breathing. It's also a good idea to have a leash and some poop bags on hand. Most airports have animal-relief areas, so make one last pit stop before getting on the plane. (Several airlines issue this warning: they will not hold the plane to wait for you and the dog.)

Did You Know?

You can bring your dog to the airport to greet or say goodbye to someone. Dogs are not allowed at the gates but you can bring them into other parts of the building, such as luggage pickup and main lobbies. Dogs must be on leashes.

Airport Dog Parks

Dogs can go first class at Phoenix Sky Harbor International Airport:

- The Phoenix airport was one of the first airports in the country to have a dog park.

- The airport dog park was born out of necessity. Airport employees noticed passengers were taking their dogs to well-manicured landscaped areas to relieve themselves. In 2003, the airport opened the Bone Yard (also a nickname for an area where old planes are stored) as a place for passengers' dogs as well as service and police dogs who patrol the area. It is a 2,000-foot-square space at Terminal 4, with a bone-shaped patch of kitty litter in the middle. Other amenities include faucets and buckets to provide dogs water for drinking and cooling off, as well as plastic mitts, shade and lighting.

- The park at the airport's busiest terminal was so successful that Sky Harbor built the Paw Pad at Terminal 3 and the Pet Patch at Terminal 2. (The airport no longer has a Terminal 1.)

- Both of the newer dog parks have upgrades: grass in the middle of the area and fire hydrants.

- The parks are a huge hit with travelers but also popular with the dogs who work in the airport, those on police patrols or those used to sniff out narcotics or explosives. With the pet parks on site, patrol dogs and their handlers no longer have to leave the airport and travel to a nearby park.

Heading to San Diego with Your Dog

All dogs go to heaven but some, if they are lucky, also go to San Diego.

First you have to get there, and that can involve either flying or driving. If you are driving, it takes about six hours, starting on I-10 West and then continuing on I-8 West. Yuma is the big exciting stop along the way. There are desolate stretches, so make sure you have enough water for you and your dog in case of any breakdowns.

Yes, it's a "fur" piece to San Diego—but it is worth it, especially for your dog. San Diego is routinely named as one of the Best Places in America for Dogs by *Dogster* magazine. The city is recognized for its off-leash parks and beaches, canine-friendly businesses and compassionate policies toward homeless animals.

Beaches

In San Diego, they don't just have off-leash dog parks—they have off-leash dog beaches, areas where your dog can run free and have a blast on the sand and in the waves.

On the beaches, general dog-park etiquette needs to be followed: If your dog needs to be leashed, use a six-foot one. Make sure your dog is healthy, licensed and vaccinated, and pick up after your dog. Leave your aggressive dog at home.

Dog Beach–Ocean Beach

With 38 acres and beautiful coastline, Dog Beach is the original dog beach and one of the most popular places in San

Diego to take your four-legged friend. It's been that way since the beach began in 1972.

The beach is open 24 hours a day, and two blocks away is the Dog Beach Dog Wash, a self-service dog wash that's been around since 1993.

Remember, not all of Ocean Beach is dog friendly—only the northern portion located at the west end of the San Diego River Floodway.

Three amigos hanging out at the beach. Photo courtesy of Jodie Snyder

Fiesta Island–Mission Bay

This is another leash-free city dog beach, but unlike the original Dog Beach, it has business hours: it's open 6:00 a.m.–10:00 p.m. every day. Fiesta Island offers sandy dunes and calmer waters, and locals say the north end is a better choice.

Dog Beach–Coronado

The dog beach in Coronado is at the most northern end of the beach next to the Naval Air Station. You and your dog get to frolic in the Pacific Ocean with the Hotel del Coronado in the background. Nice.

North Beach–Del Mar

Del Mar's North Beach is home to a lovely area of sand and surf and the annual Surf Dog Surf-a-thon. Some new rules have gone into effect: the beach from 25th Street north to the city's border with Solana Beach is now open to dogs from dawn to 8 a.m. all year.

Scoop the Poop

Many people who bring their dogs to the beach wonder if they really need to pick up their dogs' waste. They figure it can be swept away by the tide, so why bother?

There's a number of good reasons to pick up after your pooch rather than having Mother Nature do it for you:

1. Fecal coliform bacteria in seawater, courtesy of dog waste on the beach, can make people and animals very ill. In some cases, bacteria can reach levels that require the local health departments to issue swimmers' health advisories.

2. While your dog poop is laying on the beach waiting to be whisked away by the tide, it can be stepped on by other beachgoers or played with or sampled by children at the beach. Yecch, yecch, yecch.

Life After the Beach

In the very strange event that you may want to take a break from the beach, here are some other great dog things to check out while in San Diego:

- Balboa Park welcomes leashed dogs. The quiet and beautiful park is full of museums, outdoor events and gorgeous gardens—a great place to relax or throw a Frisbee with the hound.

- Otay Ranch Shopping is a totally dog-friendly shopping center with stores such as Macy's and REI. It also has a dog park right next to it. Or there's upscale Westfield Mall, which also has an adjacent Bark Park. Or Carlsbad Outlet Mall, an outdoor mall where dogs are welcome in most stores.

- 🐾 Check out the Dog Days of Summer at Petco Park, when people can bring their dogs to a Padres baseball game.

- 🐾 San Diego has a wealth of restaurants that offer patio dining and permit your well-behaved dog to join you. Some of the locals' favorites include: Dick's Last Resort, McCormick & Schmick's Seafood Restaurant–Omni Hotel, Sally's Restaurant & Bar, and Terra Restaurant.

- 🐾 Or you can take surfing or paddleboarding classes with your dog. Some instructors are affiliated with animal-rescue groups and your tuition goes to supporting their programs. Just make sure your little buddy has a life-jacket—swimming in the ocean is nothing like swimming in your pool back in Phoenix.

Kiki loving the beach. Photo courtesy of Ruth Monahan Smith

What to Take for Your Dog for a Day at the Beach

The American Kennel Club has some tips on how to make a day at the beach fun for you and your Doggy Surfin' Dude:

- **Don't drink the (ocean) water:** Don't allow your dog to drink too much seawater. It can cause diarrhea or vomiting and quickly dehydrate a dog. Bring along plenty of fresh water for your dog to drink.

- **Mind the sun:** Bring along an umbrella so your dog can get out of the sun. Dogs can get sunburned, so limit your dog's exposure and apply a zinc-free sunblock to his ears and nose 30 minutes before going outside.

- **Watch the tootsies:** Be careful not to let your dog spend too much time on the hot sand. Dogs can burn their feet just as easily as we can.

- **Be careful:** Check with lifeguards for daily water conditions. Dogs can be easy targets for jellyfish.

- **Avoid overexertion:** Swimming is a great form of exercise for dogs, but don't let them overdo it. They will be using new muscles and may tire quickly. Ditto for running on the beach.

- **Watch their step:** The beach can present many hazards for your dog. Things to watch out for include fishhooks, dead fish, garbage and broken glass.

- **Rinse, repeat:** Salt and other minerals in ocean water can damage your dog's coat, so rinse him off at the end of the day.

Crossing the Border with Your Dog

It's the closest beach to Phoenix: a mere four to five hours away, Rocky Point/ Puerto Penasco offers sun, surf and lots of great deals on shrimp.

If you want to take your dog across the border, you must have a health certificate issued and signed by an accredited veterinarian on their letterhead. The certificate must be issued within 10 days of your trip and includes info about the dog's rabies and parasite vaccinations and overall health. Veteran Rocky Point travelers say that usually border crossing guards don't ask for your dog's papers. But don't count on this. If they ask, just politely hand over the paperwork. No muss, no fuss.

There are, however, some reports that U.S. dog food has been confiscated at the border. It may be a good idea to bring a small batch of food from home and buy additional supplies at the nearby Sam's Club or Rocky Point retailers. You can always donate the leftover food to a local shelter.

Parasites are common in Rocky Point because preventive health care isn't widespread and there are large numbers of stray "street dogs," says Gilbert veterinarian Billy Griswold of Priority Pet Hospital.

In Rocky Point, your dog can pick up fleas, ticks, scabies mites, roundworms and hookworms. Even if you keep your dog away from other dogs, she can still pick up parvovirus and leptospirosis from contaminated soil and water.

The answer is not to leave Pooch at home but instead to make sure she is protected through vaccinations. Also, let your vet know that you and the dog are headed to Mexico, Griswold says.

Nancy Phelan, founder of the Animal Adoption Center of Rocky Point and advocate for thousands of the city's street dogs and cats, offers some other tips:

- Keep your dog on a leash—there are leash laws in Mexico.

- Make sure your dog has his tags, with information on how to contact you while you are out of town. Many dogs are lost during the fireworks season around July 4th.

- Purebred dogs are stolen for the reward. "I had an American actually offer $500 for his dog (a mastiff)," says Phelan. "This large reward only encourages the theft. And this owner let his dog run free!"

Heading Up North with Your Dog

In the Valley, we are lucky that we can drive a couple of hours and get to cooler climates and green forests. Communities like Flagstaff and Prescott not only offer a break from the heat, they also offer a lot of nifty hiking trails and dog parks so you and your dog can get back in touch with Nature.

Take some precautions as you and your favorite Fido head out for a trip Up North. Dr. Monet Martin of Kaibab Animal Hospital in Flagstaff, who treats a lot of vacationing Phoenix-area dogs, offers some health tips:

- **Don't overdo:** People come to northern Arizona to enjoy the great outdoors. Oftentimes, dogs get a little too excited on the trails and overdo it. Martin sees many limping dogs who have overexerted themselves. Usually they have mild sprains but sometimes they can have a torn cruciate ligaments or heat exhaustion.

- **Don't overheat:** While Flagstaff is not nearly as warm as Phoenix, the altitude and intense sun make heatstroke a common problem. Make sure to carry water and offer lots of breaks to dogs who sometimes don't know how to slow themselves down.

- **Altitude change**: As with people, the change definitely affects dogs' endurance. They tire more quickly and are more susceptible to heat exhaustion and dehydration until their bodies adapt. Dogs with pre-existing but silent or compensated-for heart or respiratory conditions may start to show symptoms at a higher altitude, such as coughing and wheezing.

- **Beware of rats:** Cabins often have rat bait put out by landlords, and dogs eat it like children eat candy. As long as owners are aware that dogs have ingested the poison, treatment is nearly always successful. It can be fatal if untreated; have a local vet's number handy so your dog can get immediate attention.

- **Beware of skunks**: It's going to be a long trip home if your dog meets up with a skunk and gets doused by the critter. Besides the horrible smell, skunk spray fumes can be very irritating to your dog's eyes or mucous membranes. Check out Martin's blog at http://kaibabvet.blogspot.com/ for a "deskunking" recipe for dogs.

- **Beware of "foxes"**: Foxtails are very common. Checking your dog's paws and coat for the botanical pests after hiking is crucial. Take him to the vet if he starts shaking his head or rubbing his eyes.

- **Be on the lookout:** Giardia is the most common intestinal parasite in Northern Arizona. If your dog has it, his symptoms can include loose, mucousy stool and vomiting. Tick-borne disease can be picked up along popular trails, so begin flea and tick prevention before going into the woods. Heartworms are more prevalent in the Verde Valley.

- **Rabies:** There have been several rabies outbreaks among Northern Arizona wildlife in recent years. Make sure your dogs are up to date with vaccinations.

"Stay"-cations

The metro Phoenix area is home to some of the country's most luxe resorts—why not take advantage of their summer room rates and get away for a little "stay"-cation? And speaking of "stay"—check to see if your four-legged friend is welcome to tag along to the Land of Luxury.

More and more hotels and resorts are becoming doggy friendly. The number of pet-friendly hotels has risen from under 2,000 to more than 40,000 since the late 1990s, according to the American Pet Products Association. It's as simple as people wanting to travel with their pets and hotels wanting to book their business.

Just a Little Prep Work

Every resort is a little different when it comes to welcoming dog guests. Some charge fees; others, like the Hotel Valley Ho and Mountain Shadows, waive them. ("So many of us consider our pets a part of the family and we want to welcome everyone," says Kristin Heggli of the properties). Some resorts welcome all types and sizes of dogs; others offer special discounts and packages. So, as with any great vacation planning, it really pays to shop around before selecting a summertime escape for you and the pooch.

Wrigley living the good life. Photo courtesy of Hotel Valley Ho

Some to-do items before getting Rover some R and R:

- 🐾 Call the resort before making reservations to confirm their pet policy.
- 🐾 Ask about pet deposits and whether they are refundable.
- 🐾 Are there weight or breed restrictions? Cleaning fees?
- 🐾 Do they provide beds, bowls and food?
- 🐾 Can your dog be left alone in the room?

A number of Scottsdale resorts go all out—right down to a "pet in room" door sign and a doggie mint on the pillow for your little buddy. The Scottsdale Convention and Visitors Bureau has a list of dog-friendly accommodations on their website, or you can check out www.happydogphoenix.com for an up-to-date list.

At the Fairmont Scottsdale Princess, visiting dogs get the "Posh Paws" treatment: a plush pet bed, food and water bowls, drip mat, squeaker toy, chewy treat and Pet in Residence door hanger. Pet-friendly rooms are also available on the ground floor next to green spaces to make "going out" easier. Upon arrival, the concierge provides dog treats and a pet packet full of recommendations for local dog parks, animal clinics for emergencies and pet-friendly hikes for recreation. Doggie day care is also available nearby. O, la, la.

Meet the House Dogs

The resort even has dogs to welcome your dogs. Bixby, a yellow Labrador retriever and Gibbs, a red golden retriever, part of the hotel chain's Canine Ambassadors, are stationed at the resort's lobby to welcome humans and canines. Both are trained service dogs. They even have their own children's book and email address for guests who want to reach out and send an "ani-mail" to the dogs.

Resort concierges offer these tips on how to make your stay perfect for all members of your party:

- **Papers, please:** Bring along all of your pet's papers, vaccine information, medications and tags with vacation contact information.

- **Plan ahead:** Stock up on the food/treats your dog is used to in order to avoid tummy troubles during your travels. (Vacation isn't the time to change up an animal's diet.)

- **Looks good in pictures:** Pack a current photograph of your dog in case he goes missing and you need to show people who you're looking for.

- **Keep 'em hydrated:** Make sure water is accessible at all times at the hotel to ensure your dog doesn't get thirsty.

- **Keep 'em happy:** Have favorite toys and treats at the ready to entertain and reward him for good behavior.

- **Stay mellow:** Have appropriate over-the-counter medication handy in case your dog becomes anxious in unfamiliar surroundings.

Bixby enjoying a resort perk. Photo courtesy of Fairmont Scottsdale Princess

Leaving Your Dog Behind

One of most frequent calls concerning pet care to the Better Business Bureau (BBB) that serves central, northern and western Arizona deals with boarding a dog while the owner is away.

Every year, BBB receives hundreds of complaints from pet owners about kennels/doggie day care. Complaints include disputes over billing as well as treatment. Owners say their pets have returned home severely dehydrated and malnourished or with fleas, ticks and even maggots.

The BBB offers these tips to find a safe place for your dog to stay:

- **Do your homework:** Check the place out with the BBB first to make sure it has e a good track record.

- **Ask around:** Ask your friends, neighbors, veterinarian or local animal shelters for recomrklinmendations.

- **Make a visit:** Check for cleanliness and smells, and evaluate the overall safety of where your dog will be staying.

- **Escape-proof:** Does your dog like to go AWOL? Ask what steps the facility takes to prevent runaways.

- **What are the accommodations?:** Will your dog come in contact with other dogs? Some places let them play together, while others separate them.

- **What's the routine?** Ask about the feeding schedule, access to water and frequency of—or fees related to—exercise.

- **Who's on staff?** Is the staff friendly? Do they interact with the pets? What is their background and experience?

- **Paperwork required?** Does the facility require pets to have proof of immunization? How do they control fleas and ticks?

- **The fine print:** Ask about the hours for drop-off and pickup and make sure you understand their billing policy.

- **In case of emergency:** Ask about what happens if there is a medical emergency.

Alternatives to Boarding

If your dog has special needs (e.g. older, poor health, behavioral problems), a professional pet sitter may be for you. Your dog can still hang out where she is most comfortable. Some pet sitters come to your house twice a day; others spend the night or take the dog home with them. Many are trained in CPR and have experience in giving medications.

Some charge $22 per 20–30 minute visit; others charge $100 for an overnight visit. Some charge extra for holidays or more than one dog. Contact the National Association of Professional Pet Sitters or Pet Sitters International for some suggestions. But nothing beats personal referrals. Also make time in your schedule for the prospective pet sitter to come to the house so you and the dog can check him out. That first get-to-know-your-dog visit should be complimentary.

Your veterinarian's office might offer boarding as well. It may not be fancy, but your dog will be monitored by professionals.

Act Fast and No Tearful Farewells

No matter which option suits you for this vacation, act fast. Good places book up; others charge last-minute-appointment fees. And if you are taking your dog to a place with other dogs, you may have to make sure she is up to date on her vaccinations.

And what about the hardest part—saying goodbye? Experts say avoid long, emotional farewells that could only upset your dog. Instead, bring back treats (lots of them!).

The Sporting Life

The Wide World of Dog Sports

Is that big lunk of a dog snoozing on the couch an athlete in hibernation? Is she sleeping so she has enough energy to race down a field, jump in the air or run an obstacle course?

The metro Phoenix area is a great place to find out. With almost unlimited sunshine and a vast network of friendly dog-sports organizations, there are a lot of places for the two of you to check out. She can get a lot of exercise and you can make some great friends. Here is just a sampling of what is available.

Agility Training

Dog agility is a dog sport in which a handler directs a dog through an obstacle course and the dog is judged for his time and accuracy. The course is chock-full of A-frames, tunnels, teeter-totters, hurdles and weave poles that look like equipment for a skiing slalom course.

Dogs run the course without benefit of leashes and handlers can't touch the dogs or offer them any treats as incentives. Handlers can only use their voices and hand signals to help their dogs navigate the course—it's more than just guiding your hungry dog through the pet food section at PetSmart.

Jumping Chollas Agility Club, in northwest Phoenix, Glendale and Peoria, is the largest agility club in Arizona, with more than 250 dogs in training.

Herding breeds, shepherds, cattle dogs and collies probably do the best in the sport because they are agile and "wired" to work under the direction of a human, according to Billie Rosen, of Jumping Chollas. There are lots of other breeds which, as a whole, also do well, she says.

Dogs who aren't healthy or easy to command or who are very large are not going to do as well.

Jumping Chollas start training puppies as young as eight weeks old, mostly with puppy play and very basic obedience training. From there, they slowly introduce the dogs to more advanced work and then some basic obstacle training.

Rosen says the time commitment for agility training is like most other sports: it takes a fair amount of time if you want to be competitive, less if you don't. Jumping Chollas encourages their members to spend 10–15 minutes a day working with their dogs.

Disc Dogs

In disc dog competitions, humans throw the disc (usually a Frisbee) and the dog zips down a field, leaps into the air and catches the disc. The team is judged on how far the dog runs to catch the disc or how much acrobatic pizzazz he shows in catching it.

Little-known Arizona connection to disc dogs: A defining moment in disc dog history occurred on August 5, 1974, when an Ohio college student and his dog, Ashley Whippet, jumped the fence at a nationally broadcast baseball game between the Los Angeles Dodgers and the Cincinnati Reds. They astonished the crowd with Ashley Whippet's abilities, but it was legendary Valley broadcaster Joe Garagiola who kept his cool and continued to announce the flying disc action on the field just like it was another day at the ballpark.

Most breeds you'll see out in disc dogs competitions are the herding breeds such as cattle dogs and border collies as well as mixed breeds who just love to fetch.

Dock Jumping

If sending your dog off a pier to land happily in the water is your idea of a good time, check out Arizona Dock Dogs. In Dock Dogs, dogs are judged by how far, how high, how fast they can retrieve toys thrown into a body of water. They can participate in events such as Big Air, Extreme Vertical and Speed Retriever. There's also the Ironman event that combines all three. The competition pool is four feet deep and the jumping platform has a special floor to promote good traction.

Whitney Lightner of Arizona Dock Dogs says all kinds of dogs can do dock jumping. If the dog knows how to swim and likes to retrieve toys, then he can join in. Breeds that are very muscular are challenged because their muscle mass tends to make them sink, but Lightner has pit bulls who have overcome that challenge.

Arizona Dock Dogs begins swimming training as soon as the puppies have their full shots and their coordination begins to kick in—at about four months. After they are a year old and have completed the necessary training, they can compete.

Interested? There are usually national and regional competitions held here during the winter.

Dog Gym

Arizona Dog Sports in Phoenix is a gym for dogs. They offer a wide range of classes for you and your dog, everything from agility training to scent training to something called the High-Energy Play Date. It's a great place for overweight dogs to lose a couple pounds or for housebound dogs to let off some steam. Remember, a tired dog is a happy dog.

Some gyms will come to you. RunBuddy Mobile offers fitness sessions to help your dog get and maintain a happy, healthy life, all in the comfort of their air-conditioned fitness unit.

Flyball

Flyball is just a hoot to watch—and the dogs who participate in it look like they are having a blast as they race down a course with small hurdles to jump over, pluck a tennis ball from a stand and race back to where they started. Your dog will be part of a team and the first team to have all four dogs run without errors wins the heat.

Casey, Flyball Grand Champion
Photo couresy of Debbie A. Maerker

Champion flyball racers can get up to some ferocious speeds, sailing around a 102-foot track in 14.4 seconds.

The dogs that do the best at flyball are those that that can focus on a ball and focus on their handler, says Carol Osterhaus of Blazin' K9s, which holds two local flyball tournaments a year in the metro Phoenix area. The herding breeds usually are excellent at it—but a border collie/Jack Russell who Osterhaus adopted from Arizona Animal Welfare League turned out to be a grand champion. Casey was a year old when Osterhaus adopted her. She was good at agility, but when Osterhaus tried her out at flyball, she was a natural at it. In fact, she was such a natural that it's her face that is in the Blazin' K9s logo.

Casey's winning ways go to show that all dogs can get involved in the sport, Osterhaus says. She's seen poodles, Jack Russell terriers and pit bulls who excel at flyball.

It's important that a dog get along with other dogs since they are part of a team. Judges will disqualify dogs who are aggressive toward other dogs at matches.

In order to compete, a dog must be one year old. However, training starts much younger with chase games and focus work. It takes patience to teach a dog the sport, Osterhaus says. Each dog learns differently and on his own schedule; training has to reflect that, she says. To begin training for flyball, it's good if a dog knows recall—that is, he comes when called, she says.

Most clubs will practice once a week for at least two to four hours. Summertime is a challenge. During the hot summer months, the Blazin' K9s start practice at 6 a.m. and finish at 8 a.m. before the heat of the day begins.

Swimming

Almost all dogs can swim with the proper training. Swimming offers the same great benefits to your dogs as it does for humans: heart-pumping, low-impact exercise for those of us who are older or overweight.

Arizona Pool Dogs trainers will teach your dog to remain calm in the water and to safely locate the stairs in your pool. They have trained dogs up to nine years old.

If your dog is a skittish swimmer, you can always put a life vest on her but make sure to keep an eye on her at all times.

Cricket loves to swim!
Photo courtesy of Brandee Waters

Fit Tips for Your Dog

Do you have a heavy hound? As America gets fatter, so do our dogs. Having a dog can be a great way for you to get exercise (nightly walk, anyone?), but it's important to ease your dog into it, especially if she is overweight or just plain old. Here are some tips from local vets:

- **Get a checkup**: Take your dog to his veterinarian for a checkup before engaging in any new exercise routines.

- **Go soft:** Dogs are just like us when it comes to their joints; softer surfaces work better for walks and runs. Consider going to grassy areas or at least the canals for your walks instead of just pounding the pavement.

- **Build up:** Going up Piestewa Peak on your first hike isn't the right first move for your little couch-potato dog. Take it slow.

- **Warm up:** Start with a walk, rather than going straight into running.

- **Bring water.**

- **Avoid the heat.**

- **You're in charge:** If your dog is slowing down, pay attention to that and adjust your outing.

- ❖ **Go short**: Frequently, two shorter trips, rather than one long walk, will help jump-start your dog's metabolism. It won't hurt yours, either.

- ❖ **Alternatives:** Too hot to walk? Think about working out in the pool, whether it is swimming, playing fetch or waging a tug-of-war game on the pool's steps. Being in the water is a good stress-free alternative for your dog's joints—but don't stay in the pool too long. And make sure plenty of fresh drinking water is available.

Happy Trails, Rover

The hiking trail is never lonely when you have your canine friend with you. And Arizona is a great place for you and the hound to explore: it has a lot of terrific trails and enough variety in climate that you can hike year-round as long as you take proper precautions.

Perhaps in recognition of this canine-hiking synergy, plenty of dog-themed hikes can be found around the state, including Lost Dog Wash Trail, a beautiful and moderate trail in the McDowell Sonoran Conservancy in north Scottsdale. Or there's Lake Pleasant's Dog Bite Site, which has Hohokam petroglyphs. Coconino County has Dog Knobs Lake, Dog Valley, Dogtown Dam. Maricopa County has Doggie Springs. You get the idea. Here are some pointers on hitting the trails with your hound.

Prepare for the Hike

It's always good to do a pre-hike, if you are taking a four-legged or even two-legged friend onto a new trail. Metro Phoenix cities and Maricopa County have great websites where you can get maps and trail info on dog-friendly hikes but there is nothing like experiencing the real thing to understand if it is suitable for any of your buddies. One thing to check for: lots of shade where you both can take breaks.

It's also important to understand your dog's limits. If the longest trek your dog has taken recently is to a food bowl, then don't go up Shaw Butte on your first hike. Try walking around your neighborhood to make sure you and your dog are ready for a longer jaunt. If you have any questions about your dog's fitness, ask your veterinarian before embarking on any big hikes. Also, use that opportunity to make sure your dog is properly vaccinated.

Pack It In

Bring enough water for you and your dog, and if you are in doubt, bring more, says Mare Czinar, a Phoenix-based hiker and travel writer. Czinar's website, ArizonaHiking.blogspot.com, is gospel for many local hikers.

A general rule of thumb is that dogs need 1.5 ounces of water per pound of body weight per day—more when it's hot, she says. So, for example, a 20-pound dog needs roughly 30 ounces of water for normal daily hydration. Double or triple that amount when hiking and stop to sip every 15–30 minutes while on the trail.

A collapsible bowl for your dog is a must, Czinar adds. Dogs need to wet the entire inside of their mouths to stay cool and hydrated. Lapping from a bottle doesn't cut it.

Don't let dogs drink from questionable water sources. Giardia (a single cell parasite) and the bacteria leptospirosis are found in contaminated pools of water and can cause intestinal distress and other health issues. Ask your vet about prevention and vaccines.

Gladys hits the trail at Brown's Ranch. Photo courtesy of Andrea King

Other good-to-have items: collapsible water bowl, doggy sunscreen, poop bags, tweezers for pulling out cactus needles and a wide-tooth comb for removing cholla. Dogs can be especially troubled by jumping cholla. They brush up against it, get stuck and then try to take the cactus out with their teeth, only to have it end up in their mouths, says Dr. Raegan Wells, a veterinarian who specializes in emergency services.

Understand the Weather

Park rangers say they see it all the time: People decide that once the weather is warm—and it's actually too warm—they take their dogs on a first-time hike. Chances are these are the same people who don't bring enough water for their dogs, either. If you think of dogs as children in fur coats, you'll realize how terribly cruel this is. It is now illegal to take your dog hiking on a city-of-Phoenix trail when temperatures top 100 degrees.

If your dog is seeking shade or lying down on the trail, stop! Shade her, give her as much water as she'd like to drink and apply water to her with a cool cloth. Get her off the trail as fast as possible and, if warranted, to the vet's office. Other warning signs of potential heatstroke:

- Excessive panting with the mouth wide open
- Seeking water
- Weakness and dizziness
- Excessive salivating

Pack the Leash

It's the law that you must have your dog on a leash no longer than six feet when in public—and it's also good common sense. No matter how well they are trained, unleashed dogs can spook other hikers, cyclists or horse riders (Phoenix-area trails can be really crowded during the prime hiking season of October through May.) Colliding with someone else on the trail is dangerous for everyone, including your dog. Also, having your dog on a leash reduces the chances he will get mixed up with rattlesnakes or coyotes. If your dog is bitten by a rattlesnake or other critter, don't panic or attempt to treat the wound yourself, as some well-meaning field operations can cause more harm than good, Czinar says. Walk or carry your dog off the trail and into the nearest emergency vet clinic. Most dogs recover just fine, she adds.

Be a Good Citizen

You and the dog should follow the general rules of the road: The slowest among us stay to the right; save the left of the trail for passing. Downhill traffic yields to uphill traffic, and it's a good practice for hikers with dogs to yield to other hikers.

Photo courtesy of Kristin Clark

Another important rule of the trail: pick up after your dog. It's common courtesy and state law. Czinar says she sees left-behind poop bags all the time on the trail, mostly as people forget to pick them up on their return trip or just mistakenly believe the "poop fairy" will handle it.

Instead of believing in the poop fairy, it's a good idea to carry out the poop yourself. Czinar suggests making your own poop tote using an empty plastic wide-mouth jar and a cheap drawstring sack. Add a couple tablespoons of baking soda (or those expensive odor-absorbing crystals) to the jar, place it in the sack and hook it to your backpack. Place poop bags in the jar and seal, she advises.

Dog-Friendly Hiking Trails

You and the hound can find a lot of terrific hikes in and near metro Phoenix. If you are looking for a road trip to boot, there are plenty of trails Up North that will make you two very happy.

Around Phoenix

- **Apache Wash:** Lovely, smooth, well-groomed trails with some shady spots. Watch out for mountain bikers, though! Part of the newer trails in city of Phoenix's Sonoran Preserve.
- **Brown's Ranch:** Easy-peasy through lush desert of McDowell Sonoran Conservancy. Perfect for new hikers and their dogs.
- **Dreamy Draw:** Trails aren't well marked but they are relatively smooth.
- **Go John:** Part of the trail is very shady and part isn't. So think ahead and either go clockwise around the trail or go counterclockwise and treat the trail as in-and-out instead of a loop. Part of Maricopa County parks—will require admission fee.
- **North Mountain Trailhead:** The path up Shaw Butte is a popular one for dogs; it's steep. but they seem to love it. North Mountain Visitor Center is super dog friendly and a good place for you and the dog to cool down, if necessary. There's a dog water bowl right underneath the indoor water fountains.
- **Spur Cross–Dragonfly:** Very simple hike through lush desert and stream beds. Part of Maricopa County parks—will require admission fee.

- **Taliesin Overlook:** Little bit more challenging but still very, very doable. Part of McDowell Sonoran Conservancy.

Out-of-Town Hiking

- **Groom Creek** near Prescott: Good trail, steep in some places and definitely a climb to the top but the views are terrific. Watch for horses.

- **Horton Creek** near Payson: Does your dog like to play in water? Babbling brook provides a quiet place to get away.

- **Parsons Trail** near Sedona: Quiet, with some water hopping. Very dog friendly.

- **Wilson Meadow at Hart Prairie** near Flagstaff: A hike that can be as short as you want it to be. Wilson Meadow offers plenty of romping room and a pond to swim in (That's for the dog, not you.).

- **Griffith Spring Trail near Flagstaff:** Another short hike that allows your dog to wade in a creek.

Cooper and Cricket are ready to hike. Photo courtesy of Brandee Waters

Sea Dogs

For a state known for its deserts, Arizona has a lot of great watering holes—more than 200 lakes and major rivers throughout the state, offering enough of the wet stuff to keep any water lover happy.

And that goes for Aqua-dogs as well. There are no laws against having your dog with you on your boat, kayak or paddleboard. Just bring some common sense, say water- and dog-loving people, and everything can be perfectly "beachy."

The best way to help your seafaring dog is to teach her to swim before boarding the boat. Practice aquatic skills slowly and gradually in your backyard pool before getting on a watercraft. Also, it really pays off to have a well-trained dog who isn't going to disappear on you while she is onshore or who won't jump off the boat for fun.

When it comes time to take your little water dog aboard, plan on being on the boat for just a short visit to get her acclimated. Dogs can experience seasickness just as they can get carsick. Sometimes dogs, especially puppies, grow out of it; other times, you may need to go to your vet for medication.

It's Best with a Vest

If all goes well with that maiden voyage, go ahead and get a life vest for your dog, even though she has been trained to swim. It will give you greater peace of mind, says Dawn Celapino, owner of Leash Your Fitness, a San Diego company that provides fitness opportunities for dogs.

Jack is a true water dog. Photo courtesy Leash Your Fitness

Celapino takes Jack, a cairn terrier, on adventures across the country, including stops at Lake Pleasant, Bartlett Lake and Prescott. Jack grew up as a surf dog and knows his way around a body of water, but Celapino always straps him into a vest. In addition to its safety features, the vest provides an easy way for Celapino to snag him out of the water, just by gripping one of the vest's strips.

To get the best-fitting vest possible, go to your local sporting goods or dog-supply store instead of shopping online.

Once you get the vest, have your dog wear it around the house to get used to it. That way, she's not being overwhelmed by getting used to the vest and the boat/kayak/paddleboard.

In addition to the vest, make sure to bring along puppy pads for on-the-water potty breaks, poop bags for shore, treats and food, medications, water bowl and lots and lots of water. Being on the water is no substitute for drinking water. It can get really hot for dogs on board under the sun.

And lake water isn't a substitute for drinking water. Keep an eye on your first mate to make sure she is not sneaking water from the side of the boat. The water can make her sick and induce her to vomit, which causes her to drink more water. Not a fun day at the lake!

Local Watering Holes

Throughout Arizona, there are terrific lakes such as Lake Powell, where you can rent dog-friendly houseboats, or you can head to western Arizona for some fun along the Colorado River. Towns like Parker also offer dog-friendly beaches.

If you are just beginning your nautical journey, consider heading to Tempe Town Lake, where dogs are welcome. Dogs are allowed on private boats, so your buddy can become your furry first mate. There is also a walking path around the lake stocked with dog water bowls and poop-bag stations.

"Bark Parks" in Metro Phoenix

Metro Phoenix has several fine dog parks, including award winners Cosmo Dog Park in Gilbert and Jackass Acres K-9 Korral in New River. No matter what neighborhood you live in, there is a dog park near you. Be sure to pack plenty of water and bring along your best manners when you go to a park.

Avondale

- Avondale Friendship Park. (Multi-use Community Park and Dog Park)
  Location: 12325 W. McDowell Road

Chandler

(No children under age 12 are allowed in the dog parks.)

- Paseo Vista Recreation Area
  Location: 3850 S. McQueen Road
- Shawnee Park
  Location: 1400 W. Mesquite
- Snedigar Sportsplex
  Location: 4500 S. Basha Road
- Nozomi Park
  Location: 250 S. Kyrene Road

"Bark Parks" in Metro Phoenix

Fountain Hills

- Desert Vista Neighborhood Park
  Location: 12925 N. Saguaro Boulevard

Gilbert

- Cosmo Dog Park
  Location: 2502 E. Ray Road
- Crossroads Park
  Location: 2155 E. Knox Road

Glendale

- Foothills Dog Park
  Location: 57th Avenue and Union Hills Drive
- Northern Horizon Park
  Location: 63rd and Northern Avenues
- Sahuaro Ranch Park
  Location: 63rd Avenue and Mountain View Road

Photo courtesy of Town of Gilbert

Goodyear

- Rosco Dog Park
  Location: 15600 W. Roeser Road

Mesa

- Countryside Park
  Location: 3130 E. Southern Avenue
- Quail Run Park
  Location: North of McDowell Road, off of Greenfield Road

New River

- Jackass Acres K-9 Korral (membership fee required)
  Location: 41635 Old Black Canyon Highway

Peoria (Dog-Friendly Areas)

- ❧ Sunnyslope Park
  Location: 9280 N. 71st Avenue

- ❧ Parkridge Park
  Location: 9734 W. Beardsley Road

- ❧ Alta Vista Park
  Location: 10631 W. Williams Road

- ❧ Scotland Yard Park
  Location: 9251 W. Scotland Avenue

- ❧ Pioneer Community Park
  Location: 8755 N. 83rd Avenue

Phoenix

- ❧ Cesar Chavez Dog Park
  Location: 7858 S. 35th Avenue

- ❧ Laveen Deem Hills Dog Park
  Location: 26606 N. Deem Hills Parkway

- ❧ Deer Valley Dog Park
  Location: 19602 N. 19th Avenue

- ❧ Esteban Park
  Location: 3345 E. Roeser Road

- ❧ Grovers Basin Dog Park
  Location: 17447 N. 20th Street, located in Grovers Basin on 20th Street at Cave Creek Road and Grovers

- ❧ Hance Dog Park
  Location: 323 W. Culver Street

- ❧ Paradise Valley Dog Park
  Location: 17642 N. 40th Street

- PetSmart Dog Park at Washington Park
  Location: 21st Avenue, north of Maryland Avenue (between Bethany Home and Glendale Avenue)

- RJ Dog Park at Pecos Park
  Location: 48th Street and Pecos Parkway (enter from 48th Street via Chandler Boulevard)

- Rose Mofford Sports Complex
  Location: 9833 N. 25th Avenue (north of Dunlap)

- Steele Indian School Park
  Location: Just off the park's parking lot on the west side of 7th Street, just north of Indian School Road

Scottsdale

- Chaparral Park's Off-Leash Area
  Location: 5401 N. Hayden Road

- Horizon Park's Off-Leash Area
  Location: 15444 N. 100th Street

- Vista del Camino Park
  Location: 7700 E. Roosevelt Street

Surprise

- Community Dog Park
  Location: 15930 N. Bullard Avenue

- Dick McComb Dog Park
  Location: 17894 W. Park Boulevard

Tempe

- Creamery Park
  Location: 8th Street and Una Avenue

- Jaycee Park
  Location: 5th Street and Hardy Drive

Happy Dog Phoenix

- Mitchell Park
  Location: Mitchell Drive and 9th Street
- Papago Park
  Location: Curry Road and College Avenue
- Tempe Town Lake
  Location: Mill Avenue and Rio Salado Parkway

Dog Park Etiquette

Dog parks provide a great opportunity for dogs to unleash some pent-up energy, but problems may arise when your pal encounters "strange" dogs. Dog-park regulars agree the most important precaution to take at the park is to keep an eye on your dog. Perhaps it is time to keep the cell phone in your pocket and concentrate on the dog? Here are some other simple safety measures to take so that both you and your dog can enjoy our terrific dog parks:

- **Know your dog**: Be honest with yourself about your dog. If he's a large dog, take him to the large-dog section. If he is a hostile or scared dog, take him to classes instead of the park. Brianna Kuna, who oversees training of shelter dogs at Arizona Animal Welfare League, suggests walking scared dogs around the outside perimeter of the park to get them used to it before entering the park. Going during off-hours is another easier way to introduce your dog to the park. Also understand that not all dogs love the dog-park action. For some, it may be just too much stimulation, she says.

- **Read the thermometer**: Hundred-degree days are hard on dogs. Go to the park in the early morning or evening.

- **Read your dog's thermometer**: If you think your dog may be sick, skip the dog park.

- **Bring water:** Sure, the park has a water fountain, but bring your own water just in case and to make sure you have some for the drive back. Also, do your best to shade your car to make it as comfortable as possible for both of you when you have to get back into it.

- **Follow the rules:** Rules vary, but generally dogs must be on-leash when entering and exiting the off-leash area, no aggressive dogs are allowed, all messes should be cleaned up, and dogs must be current on all necessary vaccinations and be controlled through voice commands.

- **Vaccinate:** Make sure you keep your dog's vaccinations up to date so he is fully protected from any disease. Diseases can be spread through direct contact between dogs, shared bowls and equipment, contaminated water, stool, insects and other methods.

- **Clean up:** Clean up after your own dog(s) and place poop in appropriate containers.

- **Keep an eye on other dogs**: Avoid contact with dogs that appear aggressive.

- **Dog parks and kids**: Your children should know about safety around dogs before they go to a dog park. Keep a close watch over them at the park.

- **Wash your hands:** Do not pet or handle a dog who appears unhealthy. If contact with an ill dog cannot be avoided, wash your hands thoroughly and change clothes (or cover your clothes) before handling your own dog or another apparently healthy dog.

- **Back off, Jack:** Do not let your puppy come into contact with other dogs' poop.

- **Check for ticks**: Check for ticks after any outside gathering and remove any ticks as soon as possible. Remove a tick by carefully using tweezers to firmly grip the tick as close to the pet's skin as possible. Then gently and steadily pull the tick free without twisting it or crushing it.
- **Shower down**: As a precaution, many dog families hose their dog down after Fido plays in Gilbert's Cosmo Dog Park Lake to prevent any infections.

Creating a Dog Park

More people and more dogs are using off-leash dog parks than ever before.

But is your dog park making the grade?

Ideally, dog parks should provide a healthy, secure space for pooches and their people. However, a poorly designed dog park can cause problems between dogs and, ultimately, between their humans, say landscape architects.

By the Numbers

The first dog park in America was opened in Berkeley, California, in 1979. Before then, dogs basically ran around; leash laws didn't exist or weren't enforced. Looking back, the decision by a city to create a space dedicated for doggie exercise may have been one of the first signs that people's attitudes were changing toward dogs; we were starting to think of them more as family members rather than creatures that just hung around.

Fastforward to today, when off-leash dog parks are the fastest-growing type of park in America's largest cities. The Trust for Public Land says the number of dedicated dog parks has grown by 40

Dogs love the lake at Cosmo Dog Park. Photo courtesy of Town of Gilbert

percent since 2009, when the nonprofit first started tracking the numbers.

Locally, over the last six years, the city of Phoenix has added four more parks because of public demand. Even with nine recognized dog parks, Phoenix is still behind other cities when it comes to play space for our best friends. According to the most current stats, Phoenix has 0.7 dog parks for 100,000 people. Compare that with Boise, Idaho, which leads the country at 6.7 parks per 100,000 people, or Las Vegas, which has 5 dog parks per 100,000 people.

What the People (and Dogs) Want

What do people want from a dog park? Shade! say Parks and Recreation officials in Gilbert, home to Cosmo Dog Park, a nationally recognized dog park.

Other needs include access to water, surface cover and safety for both canines and humans. Sometimes, thoughtful design can help fulfill those needs. Parks with easy access to parking can make it easier for dogs to enter the park in less excitable states. A long and winding path to the park may be pleasing to us, but it only heightens the dog's anticipation and energy levels. You arrive at the front gate with an amped-up dog.

Some dog parks allow dogs to come and go without being forced in a small area together, making entering and exiting the park less stressful. In addition to eliminating potential conflicts, that feature—as long as it has the right kind of gate—can prevent dogs from making an escape.

In looking to improve Cosmo, Gilbert officials are trying to solve a long-standing dog-park problem: worn-out grass. Grass, no matter what the type, disappears fast at a dog park. And when the grass goes, all that's left is a lot of dirt and mud. Reseeding has to happen and the dog park is closed while the grass tries to reclaim its turf. Gilbert is trying to split its dog park so that one area can be "off-duty" while the other takes the brunt of dogs' paws. That way, the dog park never has to shut down for maintenance.

Gilbert's Cosmo Park—A Local Standout

The Cosmo Dog Park was created through an amazing opportunity. The town of Gilbert was going to end up with large retention basins courtesy of Santan Freeway construction. After recognizing a need, civic leaders turned those potential eyesores into one of the community's most popular gathering spots.

From Day One, the park was designed to be where dogs come to play. There's a lot of color everywhere. There are fire-hydrant drinking fountains. Large dog-bowl fountains. Paw prints etched into concrete steps.

The park's focal point is a lake with a long dock where dogs can take a flying leap to happily splash into the water. The lake is surrounded by a beach, with dog-washing stations where dogs can be hosed down before heading home.

Gilbert town officials also put in exercise gear, complete with agility equipment such as climbing obstacles and tubes that were recommended by their police department's canine unit. The equipment pulls double duty—not only can the general public use it for play, but also the canine unit uses it for training.

The park is named after the most famous dog in Gilbert—the town's original police K-9, Cosmo.

Even before it opened in 2006, the park was popular. Town officials reported that curious dog lovers climbed over and under fencing to get an early peek. More than 5,000 people attended the grand opening.

And people and their dogs still keep coming. Gilbert officials say the park gets about 30,000 visits a year.

How Does Your Dog Park Compare?

Dog Fancy magazine annually ranks dog parks across the country.

To be considered, parks must have fencing, double gates and free cleanup bags. Parks are then considered based on a list of criteria including:
- Water for dogs and their people
- Shade
- Lights
- Parking availability and accessibility
- Special events

Photo courtesy of Town of Gilbert

Five Places to Take Your Dog

Think you have been everywhere with your dog? Check these out:

1. **Canals:** The Valley is blessed with a 131-mile main canal system. These canals have a long history that stretches back to the prehistoric Hohokam. As then, the canals' primary job is to deliver water to the Valley for drinking and farming. A side benefit is that the canal banks are also available for walking, jogging and bicycling. Dogs are welcome—but don't let them go swimming, because that water has certainly not been filtered.

   Some of the nicest canal sections include (look for dog-friendly restaurants along the way):

   - Arizona Canal from Cortez Park at 35th Avenue and Dunlap Avenue east to 44th Street
   - Indian Bend from Cactus Road and 40th Street. south to Indian School Road
   - Grand Canal from 23rd Avenue and Indian School Road to Papago Park

2. **Baseball games:** Chase Field is all about being "home base" for dogs. The downtown Phoenix ballpark has a special dog-friendly section that is open for many weekend

Five Places to Take Your Dog

home games. In addition, there is usually a Take Your Dog to the Game day that allows dogs in all the stands.

Be on the lookout for spring-training games that are dog friendly as well—nothing like having a ballpark hot dog with your favorite dog.

Photo courtesy of Arizona Diamondbacks

3. **Phoenix Rio Salado Habitat Restoration Project**: Located less than two miles from downtown Phoenix, the project is turning a dry riverbed/dumping ground back to its lush glory as a Sonoran wildlife and bird habitat. A welcome center offers interactive exhibits, an interpretive loop trail and connections to the Rio Salado Habitat's sixteen miles of hiking and riding trails.

   Leashed dogs are allowed only on the asphalt trails. The project staff wants to make sure dogs don't disturb progress being made at the site. The project is located at 3131 S. Central Avenue in Phoenix.

   Looking for nature and willing to take a longer drive? The Boyce Thompson Arboretum, which is an hour's drive east of Phoenix, offers plenty of Fido-friendly walking trails on its 300-acre campus that showcases Sonoran plant life.

4. **Festivals**: Every weekend from mid-January through April, there is a festival someplace in the Valley: Greek, fine art, chocolate, fitness and hot-air balloons. You name it and someone is celebrating it. If it is outside, then chances are your well-behaved, leashed dog is welcome. (One notable exception: The Arizona Renaissance Festival—ye olde dog owners leavest thy mutts at home).

5. **Farmers' markets**: The Valley has farmers' markets year-round but try to visit them with your dog in the pleasant winter and spring months. Here are just some of the markets that sell dog treats:

   - **Ahwatukee Farmers' Market:** Sundays, 8:00 a.m.–11:00 a.m., Ahwatukee Community Swim and Tennis Center, 4700 E. Warner Road
   - **Roadrunner Park Farmers' Market:** Saturdays, 8:00 a.m.–1:00 p.m., 3502 E. Cactus Road
   - **Wigwam Farmers' Market:** Sundays (November through April) 9:00 a.m.–1:30 p.m., 300 E. Wigwam Boulevard Litchfield Park

Dogs and Arizona

Digging Up Very Old Dog Bones

Want to better understand the enduring link between humans and dogs? Arizona has been an archaeological treasure trove for researchers looking to learn more about this centuries-old partnership.

In the 1940s, University of Arizona anthropologist Emil W. Haury uncovered human and animal remains and stone tools dating back to about 10,000 years ago at Ventana Cave, southwest of Phoenix. There, on what is now the Tohono O'odham Nation, Haury found remains the size of a spaniel dating back to 9500 BC.

What kind of life did that little spaniel-like creature have? Chances are she was an excellent scavenger. The desire and the ability to scavenge was what helped turn certain wolf populations into domesticated dogs. They followed camps of people as they moved through areas, eating up what the humans left behind. Scavenging became a necessary survival skill that was passed along and refined by generation and generation of wolves-turned-dogs. The little spaniel may have been a guard dog, hunting dog and possible bed-warmer, and but she was undoubtedly a full-time garbage collector (and eater).

When Haury made his discovery, the Arizona remains were considered to be the oldest evidence of a domesticated dog in North America. His find was breathlessly reported in a 1949 *Popular Mechanics* magazine article entitled "Cave Gives Up Its Secrets."

Did the Hohokam Have Dogs?

Metro Phoenix has its own share of ancient canines. The Hohokam, who built miles of sophisticated canals around the Phoenix area as far back as 1 AD, also had dogs with them. The Hohokam farmed this area until around 1450; then they mysteriously disappeared. The Akimel O'odham are considered the successors to the Hohokam in the Phoenix area.

Phoenix is lucky to have Pueblo Grande, the site of Hohokam adobe and stone ruins at 44th and Washington Streets. Archaeologists have studied this area since the 1880s, looking for clues about the Hohokam's ways of life and their disappearance. The city of Phoenix has preserved the site's central portion since 1924; two major archaeological investigations have been done at Pueblo Grande, one from 1929 to 1981 and the other in 1989.

Over the years, more than a dozen dog burials have been excavated from Pueblo Grande, and the presence of bones of young dogs suggests that the Hohokam may have raised dogs at the site. Many researchers have concluded that dogs were pets as well as hunting companions, and there is no evidence that the Hohokam—unlike other tribes—ate their dogs, according to *Desert Farmers at the River's Edge: The Hohokam and Pueblo Grande* by John P. Andrews and Todd W. Bostwick.

Companions Forever?

The 1989 Pueblo Grande dig found fifteen dog burials, probably dating back to 1150 to 1450 AD, near or within the human burial groups.

These fifteen burials were the most ever recovered from a Hohokam site. From the large number of burials, archeologists inferred just how important domestic dogs were to Hohokam society. There is evidence that the dogs were fatally shot with arrows rather than being allowed to die from natural causes. That discovery led researchers to believe that the dogs may even have been killed upon the deaths of their owners and buried near their human companions, according to Steven R. James and Michael S. Foster writing for the Center for Desert Archaeology at the University of Arizona.

Next Life Friends

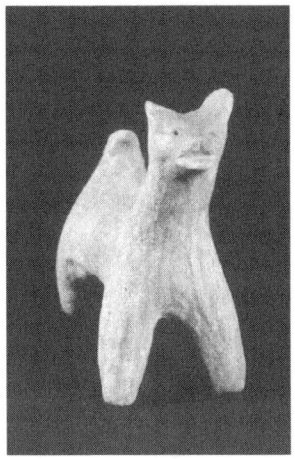

Dog figurine unearthed at Pueblo Grande. Photo courtesy of Pueblo Grande Museum

In addition to the dog burials, the Pueblo Grande excavations found an unusual cache of six intact ceramic dog figurines that had details such as erect ears and upright and slightly hooked tails. The figurines were found in a pithouse (a single-room dwelling) amid shards of other shattered figurines. Archaeologists believe the dog figurines were meant to be placed with dead persons to accompany them on the journey to the Next Life, the shards indicating that some figurines were broken as an acknowledgment of something ending, possibly the release of a spirit.

Throughout the Southwest, entire dogs or dog skulls were frequently included in human burials but the practice became less common over time, according to Dody Fugate of the Museum of Indian Arts and Culture in Santa Fe. For example, evidence of burials of dogs the size of a German shepherd and a spaniel in southern Arizona date back to 1200 to 800 BC.

After the arrival of Europeans, who brought their Christian concept of "man holding dominion over the animals," many tribes' perception and valuation of dogs appears to have changed, Fugate wrote in an article for the Center for Desert Archaeology. Instead of being respected as spiritual guides for the Next Life, dogs were and are now seen more as "bothersome hangers-on and individual pets," she wrote.

Dog Scholar: Stanley J. Olsen

Anyone who has ever wondered how their sofa-loving hound evolved from a wolf in the forest has to thank Stanley J. Olsen of the University of Arizona for his groundbreaking research into the evolution of dogs.

Known as a founding father of zooarchaeology, Olsen was professor of anthropology at the University of Arizona and curator of zooarchaeology at the Arizona State Museum from 1973 until his retirement in 1997.

Stanley J. Olsen was one of the founding fathers of zooarchaeology. Photo courtesy of University of Arizona

When Olsen began his work, there were two camps—archaeologists who studied human bones, and zoologists, who studied animal bones—and not a lot of meeting in the middle, he told Jon Franklin for Franklin's book *The Wolf in the Parlor*.

Undaunted, Olsen tackled the fledgling field of zooarchaeology to better understand the histories of both animals and humans. The field has evolved into researching the past relationships between humans and animals on topics such as human diet, domestication of animals, economics, trade and use of animals in rituals.

How Dogs Came to Be

Olsen had a profound influence on how researchers look at the evolution of dogs. His 1985 *Origins of the Domestic Dog* is considered a Bible of sorts for archaeologists doing fieldwork and identifying nonhuman remains. Olsen, for example, looked at skulls for signs such as an overall reduction in tooth size to better ascertain the evolution from hunter wolves to more domesticated dogs.

Olsen believed that different breeds of dogs likely evolved from different wolf populations. Large dogs, for instance, descended from large European wolves, while smaller dogs came from smaller wolf breeds in Asia.

Olsen recognized the value of his work, saying that he believed the domestication of animals was as critical to shaping humankind as the development of agriculture and fire. Nonetheless, he told Franklin, research money was often hard to come by.

In the Field

Olsen frequently wrote about discoveries in Arizona, bringing additional insight to findings such as dog mummies in Marsh Pass in Northern Arizona or dog skeletons near Kayenta with bones dating back to 1100 AD.

And he had his share of Indiana Jones–type adventures, going into Colombia, Belize, China, Tibet, India, Italy, Cyprus and Nepal for fieldwork. Olsen, however, postponed one long-sought-after trip to Leningrad to stay home to care for his seriously ill dog. The canine expert told a newspaper reporter that he loved all dogs but preferred mixed breeds because they more closely resembled the first versions of domesticated dogs.

Dogs in Early Phoenix History

As four-legged adventurers, dogs were instrumental in taming the Old West: protecting the homestead from animal and human predators, herding livestock and tracking down game.

As the area known as Pumpkinville changed into Phoenix and grew from a speck in an inhospitable desert to the nation's fifth-largest city, dogs got a ground-floor seat to watch the transformation. Although early settlers' lives were far different from ours today, their attitudes toward dogs appear to be not as different as you would think.

Two boys and a dog playing in or around Phoenix. Photo courtesy of Arizona State Archives

The End of Pumpkinville

In 1846, Mormons who were Mexican-American War veterans started farming along the Gila and Salt Rivers, eventually setting up the towns of Mesa, Florence and Safford; they also bestowed the name "Pumpkinville" to the area west of them.

Jack Swilling, a jack-of-all-trades—prospector, saloon owner, farmer, rancher, politician and the area's first postmaster and justice of the peace—is credited with having the idea of changing the area's name.

But many believe it was "Lord" Darrell Duppa, possible son of a well-regarded English family, Apache fighter, miner, farmer and intellectual who could speak five languages, who actually gave Phoenix its name. Among his other attributes—Duppa had dogs.

In his 1892 book *On the Border with Crook*, Captain John G. Bourke describes the stage station that Duppa ran in what is now New River—it was a place where dogs were as plentiful as guns: "The dwelling itself was nothing but a ramada, a term which has already been defined as a roof of branches; the walls were of rough, unplastered wattle work, dirt floor, long, unpainted table of pine, which served for meals or gambling.... There is hardly any use to describe the rifles, pistols, belts of ammunition, saddles, spurs and whips, which lined the walls...they were just as much part and parcel of the establishment as the dogs and ponies were."

Despite those hardscrabble accommodations, people came to the Salt River area and settled. In 1870, Phoenix was officially established as a town. Refinements followed; a schoolhouse, telegraph office and bank were built.

The Dog as Diversion

Fort McDowell during this time flourished as an Army camp. Many histories mention the large number of dogs that hung around the camps, scavenging for items. Fort McDowell was no exception: soldiers and Native Americans alike would get one of the plentiful dogs and tie a tin can to his tail to break up the monotony of camp life.

Some Army dogs were better regarded. In her memoir of the state in the 1870s, *Vanished Arizona*, Martha Summerhayes writes about how one seasoned Army major reacted to his dog's "suicide." Apparently, "Pete," a red setter, "fixed his eye upon a distant range of mountains, and ran without turning, or heeding any call, straight as the crow flies, toward them and death. We never saw him again; a ranchman told us he had known of several other instances where a well-bred dog had given up in this manner," Summerhayes wrote.

Summerhayes and her husband attempted to comfort the distraught major by bringing a quail dinner to him in his tent that night. The major said to leave it on the table and he would get up and try to eat it. When he did, he was too late. The Summerhayeses greyhound had noiselessly followed his master and snagged the quail for himself, Summerhayes wrote.

The age-old problem of dogs getting into food was not limited to Army camps.

Phoenix's first town baker, J. Bauerlein, was brilliant enough to use a small furnace made of adobe bricks for his oven. But one day in 1872, the popular baker had to print this notice to the public:

"On Tuesday last the town had no bread and the baker had a holiday because an innocent dog upset the yeast the evening before."

After Phoenix became a city in 1881, civic leaders successfully lobbied for a larger railroad presence and got a line heading east to El Paso and west to Los Angeles. More businesses followed and Phoenix responded by building one of the first electric-power-generating plants in the West, creating a Valleywide streetcar line and opening a hospital and a public library.

The Dog as Landmark

In 1888, business partners Talbot and Hubbard opened their hardware store in the Commercial Hotel in what is now downtown Phoenix. To distinguish their store from other bustling storefront businesses, they commissioned a life-sized iron statue of a mastiff that was on the Hubbard family's coat of arms. For more than 30 years, the dog was wheeled out in front of the store every day by the same employee. It became a favorite landmark and ersatz toy for children to climb on. In fact, the store used the phrase "At the Sign of the Dog" for its advertising for many years. Native Americans on nearby reservations never referred to the establishment as the Talbot and Hubbard store; they called it the Dog Standing Store. In 1929, the store changed hands and the mastiff statue was part of the deal. The dog that was part guidepost and part playground toy was last seen in front of the A. J. Bayless Cracker Barrel Country Store.

The Dog as Public Enemy

In 1899, Phoenix became the territorial capital after trying to show the world it had outgrown its Wild West roots and was a dignified, cultural city.

As part of this progressive campaign, in 1896, the editors of the city's newspaper *The Republican* fought against the shooting of unlicensed dogs on the street by an executioner hired by the city council, according to *All the Time a Newspaper: The First 100 Years of the* Arizona Republic.

The public dog executions ended a year later, when a dog belonging to a prominent citizen living outside the city roamed into town and was shot. The newspaper gave a gripping account of how a "large, fine looking, intelligent black dog was gunned down by a city-paid killer" right outside a pharmacy on north First Avenue. Thereafter, dogs were captured and then killed out of public sight.

Public safety and dogs seemed to be a long-standing issue in Phoenix. In 1893, the city council decided that dogs needed to be muzzled during June, July, August and September. Unmuzzled dogs would become "prey of the dog catcher," the *Republican* warned. And dogs were a problem less than a year later, when the paper reported that "Little Jimmie" Bridges had been attacked by a vicious dog at the end of the streetcar line in Tempe.

Others were already more sensitive to the plight of animals around them. Katherine Born, granddaughter of the wife of Morris Goldwater (Barry Goldwater's father), talked about what happened when one of her favorite dogs was blinded in one eye by boys trying to hit pigeons with their slingshots.

"Animal lover that I am, Patty (the dog) and I fell in love....Patty visited (me) regularly. How he knew where we were I don't know, but he came to see us frequently. And that's how he managed to be in the wrong place at the wrong time when they were shooting pigeons."

Protecting dogs seemed to be on the mind of Arizona's territorial leaders as well. In 1901, they thought it necessary to fine people for poisoning unclaimed dogs. Fines could range from $5 to $50.

Boy Scouts enjoying some time with a dog, circa 1910. Photo courtesy of Arizona State Archives

Representing the Dogs

In 1912, Arizona became a state, and with the creation of the Roosevelt Dam, Phoenix became an important agricultural and cotton center. In the 1930s, the Depression came, spurring civic leaders to spend more energy attracting tourists to the area. At this time, Phoenix and Arizona were able to send some stellar politicians to represent the fledgling state. The names that we now use for streets and landmarks first belonged to them.

Territorial leader Lew Collins and his dog in Phoenix, circa 1908. Photo courtesy of Arizona State Archives

Isabella Greenway, the first U.S. congresswoman in Arizona's history—and namesake for Greenway Road—in 1936 took time from her congressional schedule to defend the honor of Great Danes. Greenway was familiar with the breed because she had been given one as a gift from President Franklin Delano Roosevelt. Greenway was speaking up for "Hamlet,', a Washington hostess's Great Dane accused of knocking down small dogs and general misbehavior. Hamlet was an excellent animal and did not cause any trouble, Greenway told the press. What about her own Great Dane? He was back on the ranch in Arizona because he did not behave well enough to stay in the capital, she said.

In concluding, Greenway offered this sage advice: "Dogs are like people. Some are dependable and some are not."

Dogs in Early Phoenix History

Dogs and Politics

Presidential candidate and Arizona senator, Barry Goldwater enjoys some downtime with Cyclone III, circa 1964. Photo courtesy of Getty Images

The connection between canines and politicians continued to be strong throughout Arizona's history. Arizona's own Barry Goldwater, Phoenix city councilman, five-term U.S. senator and presidential candidate, had his beloved bulldogs. While running for president in 1964, Goldwater was asked by reporters why his bulldog, Cyclone III, had a gold tooth. It wasn't anything like his opponent Lyndon B. Johnson's pulling of his beagles' ears, Goldwater explained— it was just that the dog had bitten on something hard and broke off a tooth. A dentist who was a family friend obliged by giving Cyclone a little something extra. Goldwater liked to boast that Cyclone was the only bulldog in Arizona with a gold tooth, *Life* magazine reported.

Dick of Arizona: Mining Town Mascot

Dogs of the Old West did more than follow cattle trails or hang around the old homestead. They were fixtures in the mining towns and camps that sprung up throughout Arizona as miners searched for gold, then silver, and finally copper. Miners relied on dogs for companionship as well as protection of their hastily arranged and hardscrabble camps.

The 1887 story "Dick of Arizona" by C. H. Buffett in *Outing* magazine told the story of Dick, a dog who apparently was the mascot of Globe, the mining town about 90 miles east of Phoenix. *Warning: this story may be a tall tale.*

Dick, according to the storyteller, was a pug who was 8 inches high and 16 inches around. Despite his diminutive size, he was willing to take on any dog that came into his town. He once fell down a mineshaft and was rescued by a miner who gave him beer to help him get better. It did the trick and Dick made a full recovery. After then, Dick would get a small glass of beer now and then from the friendly miners.

For two or three days, Dick didn't have any beer, and he jumped into the mineshaft again. This time, however, the fall killed him. He was given a first-class funeral with a little coffin and an epitaph reading that Globe mourned Dick. "We had a lots of men shot here without half the mourning there was for Dick," an old miner told Buffett.

From Africa with Love: The Bill O'Brien Story

Bill O'Brien of Paradise Valley was a true Arizona hero: cowboy, rancher, businessman, community leader. He helped create the Phoenix Irish Cultural Center and, through his foresight, Camelback Mountain became part of the Phoenix Mountain Preserve instead of just another subdivision site.

He was also responsible for introducing Rhodesian Ridgebacks to the United States.

O'Brien was buying wool in South Africa in 1949 when he first met the athletic short-haired breed with the distinctive crest down its back. As a buyer, O'Brien frequently traveled across the South African continent, leaving Sada, his wife, behind, and he worried about her safety. He heard about the ridgebacks' bravery and decided they would provide security for her while he was away buying wool from the ranchers.

O'Brien contacted the president of the South African Rhodesian Ridgeback Club, Major T. R. Hawley, founder

Sada O'Brien with Rhodesian Ridgebacks. Photo courtesy of the O'Brien family

of the Rhodesian Ridgeback Club of Rhodesia, who handpicked three dogs for him and Sada.

O'Brien was initially drawn to the breed for the dogs' protective natures, but he also learned that they were excellent hunters and good-natured family dogs.

In 1950, the O'Briens stepped off the gangplank of the *African Rainbow* in Boston Harbor with his cargo of wool and the first three registered Rhodesian Ridgebacks in the United States—Tchaika, Caesar and Zua.

Before leaving Africa, O'Brien had contacted the Cape Town, South Africa, paper to announce his plans of introducing the breed to the United States. A newspaper photographer came as they were boarding to take an iconic photo of Sada holding the three dogs aboard the ship. Although Sada was reluctant to have her photo taken, the photograph hung prominently in the O'Briens' home for many, many years.

Once back in the States, O'Brien began the painstaking work of getting the breed recognized by the American Kennel Club.

O'Brien had binders and binders of evidence of the bureaucracy involved in getting the AKC to recognize the breed. Along the way, he also started the first national club, the Rhodesian Ridgeback Club of America.

In 1956, the AKC finally recognized the Rhodesian Ridgeback, the first new breed recognized in a decade. It was the 112th breed to be recognized overall.

In an issue with Harry Truman on the cover, *Life* magazine covered the news with a three-page article and photo spread of the O'Briens with their beloved dogs. Since 1949, the family had at least one Rhodesian Ridgeback in their home at all times and never regretted a moment of it.

"They are truly a very fine breed of dog for families and ranchers," O'Brien said in a 2012 interview.

Editor's note: Bill O'Brien passed away in 2015. He is sorely missed.

Buckey O'Neill: Hero and Dog Lover

Newspaper publisher, mayor, Rough Rider, Buckey O'Neill did it all—and, apparently, he was a dog lover to boot.

Around 1895, the well-known Arizonan stopped long enough in his storied travels to get his dog, Gimlet, photographed somewhere in Prescott, the town that admired O'Neill's heroic exploits so much that they put a bronze statue of him in front of their courthouse.

O'Neill didn't start out as a hero. Languishing in Washington, D.C., he decided to head West and arrived in Phoenix, riding a burro, in 1879. He was quickly hired as a printer by the *Phoenix Herald*. By late 1880, he decided to try his luck in boomtown

Gimlet, Buckey O'Neill's dog, was photographed in Prescott around 1890. Photo courtesy Arizona State Archives

Tombstone, where he joined the likes of Wyatt and Virgil Earp in pre–O.K. Corral shoot-out days.

O'Neill found work at the *Tombstone Epitaph* but got restless again and eventually moved north to Prescott, where he found his almost-destined fame and glory.

In Prescott, he began his own newspaper, *Hoof and Horn*, a paper for the livestock industry. He became captain of the Prescott

Grays in 1886, the local unit of the Arizona Militia. He directed search-and-rescue operations when Walnut Dam collapsed in 1890, killing more than 100 people in what was Arizona's greatest natural disaster. He was part of a four-man posse that captured a band of train robbers. But the brave and dashing O'Neill had a more refined side as well: he fainted when a convicted murderer was hanged.

After completing good deed after good deed, O'Neill was unanimously elected mayor of Prescott.

A couple of years later, it seemed like he was finally going to have some financial security. In 1897, after years of speculating on mines, he sold a group of claims near the Grand Canyon to Back East investors. He eventually went to work for them as a director.

Rough Riders and "Cuba"

But O'Neill's restless spirit resurfaced. In 1898, war broke out between the United States and Spain. O'Neill joined Teddy Roosevelt's Rough Riders as leader of Northern Arizona's Company A in the Spanish-American War.

Uttering statements such as "an officer should never take cover" and acting in a correspondingly brave fashion, Captain O'Neill was the regiment's most popular officer, according to Marshall Trimble, Arizona's state historian.

Even though he traveled to Cuba's warfront, O'Neill still managed to be around a dog. The Rough Riders picked up, in addition to a mountain lion and eagle, "a rather disreputable but exceedingly knowing little dog, named Cuba," according to Roosevelt's memoirs. Corporal Cade C. Jackson of Troop A from Flagstaff apparently snagged the dog from a railcar to take to the front. Cuba, who was said to have the personality of a Yorkie, entertained solders, howling as the military band played. It was also reported that Cuba followed the troops into battle, disappearing when the shooting started and returning when the smoke cleared.

Buckey O'Neill: Hero and Dog Lover

O'Neill did not survive the Spanish-American War. At Las Guasimas, he was shot by a sniper as he walked the line shouting out encouragement to his frightened troops. Cuba, however, survived and at the end of the war was given to an Arizona Territory ranger, with whom he lived for 16 more years, according to Douglas Brinkley in "Wilderness Warrior: Theodore Roosevelt and Crusade for America."

Cuba, one of the mascots of the Rough Riders, along with mountain lion Josephine, another mascot. Photo courtesy of Harvard College Library

State Dogs

Arizona state bird? *Cactus wren*
Arizona state neckware? *Bola tie*
Arizona state mammal? *The ringtail*
Arizona state dog? *None*

Arizona seems to be in mainstream when it comes to not having a state dog. In fact, according to Stanley Coren, nationally known dog expert, only 12 states have designated dogs:

- **Alaska:** Alaskan Malamute (2010)
- **Louisiana**: Louisiana Catahoula Leopard Dog (1979)
- **Maryland:** Chesapeake Bay Retriever (1964)
- **Massachusetts:** Boston Terrier (1979)
- **New Hampshire**: Chinook (2009)
- **North Carolina**: Plott Hound (1989)
- **Pennsylvania:** Great Dane (1965)
- **South Carolina**: Boykin Spaniel (1985)
- **Texas:** Blue Lacy (2005)
- **Virginia:** American Foxhound (1966)
- **Wisconsin:** American Water Spaniel (1985)

Your Happy Dog's Medical Care

Dogs Get It Too: Valley Fever

People who live in the Phoenix area for any amount of time are at risk for getting Valley Fever, a fungal infection of the lungs that in a small number of cases can be fatal. A Valley Fever infection happens after someone inhales dust contaminated with the fungus. Dogs are just as at risk for getting Valley Fever, says Lisa Shubitz, a veterinarian and researcher at the University of Arizona Valley Fever Center of Excellence.

Shubitz has her own story about how dangerous Valley Fever can be to dogs. In October 1998, Arrow, her eight-month-old whippet, developed a high fever. After more than a month of Arrow having a high fever for unknown reasons, Shubitz found out she had Valley Fever. For two more months, the dog received high doses of oral medicine but her fever continued and her appetite was next to nothing. At the end of January, in desperation, Shubitz gave Arrow an intravenous drug. After two weeks, there was improvement, but it took nine months of medicine and hand-feeding by Shubitz before Arrow was healthy again.

Here are some answers to the most commonly asked questions about Valley Fever:

How dangerous is Valley Fever?

About 30 percent of dogs who inhale Valley Fever spores develop the disease, which can have complications that range from very mild to severe and occasionally fatal. Approximately 60,000 Arizona dogs get sick annually, researchers believe. Valley Fever is not contagious, so if your dog gets it, that doesn't mean you or other animals in the house will get it. But it is a good idea for everyone to get checked out because you share the same environment.

What are the symptoms?

The most common early symptoms are:
- Coughing
- Fever
- Weight loss
- Lack of appetite
- Lack of energy

When the infection spreads outside the lungs, it can cause lameness and other medical conditions:
- Swelling of limbs, lymph nodes and testicles
- Back-of-neck pain
- Seizures and other manifestations of brain swelling
- Soft abscess-like swelling under the skin
- Nonhealing or oozing sores
- Eye inflammation with pain or cloudiness
- Unexpected heart failure in a young dog

Sometimes a dog will skip the first signs of an infection and only develop the more serious symptoms.

How is Valley Fever treated?

After a diagnosis confirms your dog has Valley Fever, the dog will be put on medications that she may be on for years.

The good news is that most dogs on medications do recover, especially with early diagnosis and intervention. Dogs with only lung infections have the best prognosis for recovery and usually respond the quickest to treatment.

Those with more serious symptoms can respond well to medication and lead normal lives. A small group must take medication for life, and a very small number, unfortunately, die of Valley Fever. Valley Fever cases in dogs can be costly as well as heartbreaking. Owners can spend at least $2,000 on diagnosis, treatment, and follow-up, Shubitz estimates.

How can I prevent my dog from getting Valley Fever?

The spores that cause Valley Fever live in dust, which is certainly plentiful around the Phoenix area. In fact, two-thirds of all cases of Valley Fever in the United States happen in Arizona. Here are some prevention tips:

- Reduce the dirt and dust in your dog's environment by planting grass or layers of gravel.
- Encourage him not to dig or sniff around rodent holes.
- Keep him inside more than outside.
- Keep him inside during dust storms.

Do certain breeds tend to become infected or have more severe symptoms?

Boxers, Australian shepherds, Doberman pinschers, Scottish terriers, beagles and pointers tend to be more susceptible.

"In my personal experience, boxers and boxer crosses, indeed, tend to have terrible disease that is hard to treat," Shubitz said. "The beagles I have treated also seem to be hard to treat."

Why do dogs tend to get Valley Fever more frequently than cats?

Shubitz said no one really knows why there is one case of Valley Fever in cats for every 50 cases seen in dogs. Here are some common theories:

- 🐾 Cats can combat the fungus earlier than dogs, which means fewer cats develop the illness.

- 🐾 Cats don't have dogs' penchant for deeply sniffing their entire world, especially dirt that harbors the spores. ("But that doesn't account for very sick Yorkies who have probably barely ever had their paws touch dirt, so I am guessing there is a differential susceptibility between the species," Shubitz said.)

How long have we known about dogs getting Valley Fever?

The first report of Valley Fever in a dog was in 1940; it was reported by a Tucson physician who discovered it in his own Great Dane.

What about the future?

Researchers at the Valley Fever Center for Excellence are working on a vaccine for both humans and canines. They hope to first perfect the vaccine on dogs before using it on humans.

When Your Pooch Is Hurt

Would you know what to do if your dog needed first aid or CPR?

You can find several places to take first aid classes for pets in the Phoenix metro area. A popular one is the Pet Tech program offered at Diamond Cut Pet Spa by Malinda Malone. The course, taken by professional dog sitters and concerned owners, allows pet guardians to become certified and more knowledgeable about what to do in case of a pet emergency.

The American Red Cross also offers classes and sells a comprehensive first aid booklet that is a good addition to your home's library.

Pet Tech's course provides the basics of CPR/pet first aid and reinforces the idea that the best thing to do with an injured animal is to get him to a veterinarian as soon as possible. The course, which lasts almost five hours, also goes through drills to help you learn how to respond to emergency situations and perform CPR and rescue breathing.

The Pet Tech class allows people to practice on a stuffed dog. Your homework, of course, is to practice on your own dog and become very comfortable with the information.

Here are just some basics taught in the Pet Tech class. This is in no way a substitute for the multi-hour course taught by trained professionals.

- **Get to know your dog.** Everyone should do the Snout-to-Tail Wellness Assessment at least every other month. This way you will find any changes in your pet's health. Get your dog used to being touched and occasionally checked over for vital signs. It will make trips to the vet a lot easier.

- **Take the pulse:** You can feel for your dog's pulse in the femoral artery of the groin. Not sure where that is? The next time your dog rolls over for a tummy rub, check the inner portion of her back leg. The best place to check her heartbeat is where her left elbow touches her chest. Heart and pulse rates vary by age and size of dog.

- Check for fever: Taking your dog's temperature rectally is really no fun for any of the parties involved. Use a pediatric digital thermometer that can be found in a drugstore and lubricate it with petroleum jelly. The dog's temperature should be between 101 and 102.5 degrees.

- **In the pink:** Gums are a good place to gauge your dog's health. You are looking for gums that are nice and pink.

- **Strings attached?** If you see a string or unknown object coming out of your dog's back end, take her to the vet. The item could be wrapped within the intestines and you may hurt your dog if you attempt to pull the item out.

- **In case of choking:** If your dog is choking, resist the urge to pat her on the back. Give her a small amount of time to cough it out. If that doesn't work, and she stops coughing, place your hands on either side of her chest and thrust inward and get ready to take her to the vet immediately. Dogs are three times more likely than cats to choke.

- **Get a grip:** If you have to pull out something slimy from your dog's mouth, use a paper towel or cloth towel to help you get a better grasp on it.

- **In case of poisoning:** Call your vet or a veterinary emergency center immediately. They can walk you through immediate steps. And make sure to collect any leftover packaging of what the dog ingested as well as any vomit for the vet to inspect for clues.

- **Seizures:** Seizures are more common in dogs than in cats. It's important that you remain calm while the dog is having a seizure. Don't restrain the dog; a lot of people get bitten trying to do so. Record how long the seizure lasts and get your dog to the vet.

- **Use restraint judiciously:** When deciding if you need to restrain a dog, realize that using the least restraint possible is preferred but also remember that your pet is in pain and not her usual loving, gentle self. Make sure you speak in a calm voice and move smoothly if you decide to muzzle your dog. Don't muzzle a dog if the dog is choking, vomiting, experiencing breathing problems or having a seizure.

What's in Your Doggy First Aid Kit:

Designate a special day to check your kit every year—say, your dog's birthday, the anniversary of when the dog arrived at your house or some other day that is easy to remember. Malinda Malone of Diamond Cut Pet Spa in Ahwatukee suggests these items for your dog's first aid kit.

Use a sturdy toolbox for your kit.

- Contact info for your vet (in very legible writing)
- Contact info for the nearest emergency hospital
- Absorbent compresses in different sizes
- Adhesive tape
- Antibiotics (triple)
- Comb (to comb out cactus needles)
- Digital thermometer (check batteries often)
- Eyedropper
- Flashlight (small)
- Gauze pads
- Gauze rolls
- Handwipes
- Hydrogen peroxide (3-percent solution)
  Have it around in case your dog needs to throw up. Always contact your vet for instructions. Have two pre-measured doses on hand. Administer the second one if the first one doesn't work in 10 minutes. Don't use syrup of ipecac.

- Muzzle and leash (It's a good idea to have more than one leash.)
- Needle-nose pliers
- Non-latex gloves
- Petroleum jelly
- Photo of you and your dog for identification purposes
- Plastic bags for cleaning up or samples
- Q-tips
- Sanitary napkins (great for absorbing liquids)
- Small pair of bandage scissors
- Syringe
- Store-brand equivalent to Benadryl for allergic reactions. Use liquid gels because they are easier to digest. Use only medications marked for allergies.
- Towel or blanket
- Triangular bandages
- Tweezers

Vetting Your Vet

Your vet is your partner in your dog's health care and it's terrific for your peace of mind when you have complete confidence in your veterinarian/partner.

The Arizona State Veterinary Medical Examining Board, which monitors more than 2,200 licensed vets in the state, is a good place to start when checking out your existing or prospective doggy doctor.

You can visit their website at www.vetboard.az.gov, which lists vets who have been disciplined by the state board. Or you can call them at (602) 364-1PET (1738) and talk with a real person to find out the straight scoop.

Board staff can tell you if a veterinarian has had any complaints or if disciplinary action has been taken against the doctor. If your veterinarian has had disciplinary action, the staff will inform you over the phone but they won't give you the details. It is up to you to pursue the matter or file a public-records review request.

Other suggestions for selecting a veterinarian:

- **Select one before you need one.** Avoid that last-minute panic and any haphazard choices.
- **Check out the facility without your dog.** You may have your hands full when taking your dog to the vet: either

your dog is way too friendly or he is dragging his heels in the parking lot. Nose around the facility beforehand for its cleanliness, staff interaction and levels of training.

- **Look for the AAHA seal:** The seal is from the American Animal Hospital Association, a voluntary accrediting association for animal hospitals.

- **After-hours call?** Your dog is no nine-to-fiver and when she gets sick it can be anytime, anywhere. Ask how your vet covers after-hours emergencies.

- **What are your charges?** When it comes to money, we sometimes get embarrassed about inquiring about the costs of services. Just politely ask what the average cost of a checkup is. You can explain that you are not necessarily looking for a bargain but you want to make sure you can budget for regular veterinary expenses.

Most of the complaints filed with the state board deal with communication issues, so board staff strongly recommend selecting a veterinarian who you can easily talk with.

Also, the board always encourages people to get second opinions if they have any qualms about the diagnosis given to their dogs. The board also certifies veterinary technicians, who perform a lot of hands-on services for your dog. Certified or not, every technician or veterinary assistant should be supervised by a licensed veterinarian who is responsible for them.

Health Insurance for Your Dog

Increasingly, companies are marketing pet health insurance to dog owners and even some employers are offering it as part of their benefits packages.

But is pet insurance a good deal?

The jury is still out: *Consumer Reports* believes it only makes sense if you expect large veterinary bills, which are increasingly commonplace as veterinary care becomes more sophisticated: pets now get CT scans and MRIs, go to cardiologists and neurologists and get chemotherapy to fight cancer.

Aja Manahan, practice manager of North Kenilworth Veterinary Care in Phoenix, thinks pet insurance coverage is definitely worth investigating. Too many times, she has seen people devastated about not being able to afford their dog's medical care. "There is such a special bond between us and our dogs and we want to take care of them no matter what."

Pet vs. People Insurance

In some ways, people and pet insurance are very similar: each has deductibles, co-pays and premiums. But there is one major difference, Manahan says. Pet insurance usually requires that people pay the vet bill first and then the insurer reimburses them.

Organizations ranging from the ASPCA (American Society for the Prevention of Cruelty to Animals) to private insurance companies now offer plans that can include everything from preventive care to behavioral therapy. Generally speaking, dog-insurance premiums are around $20 a month but can go as high as $65 for really comprehensive coverage.

There's a wide variety of dog owners out there, and there can be a plan to fit each one of their individual needs, Manahan says. And it pays to read the fine print, say consumer advocates:

- **Talk with your veterinarian:** Ask them which pet insurance they like best. Have they seen pet insurance policies that include surprise "exclusions"? For instance, some pet insurance policies exclude pre-existing conditions, so if your pet was ill in 2018, those conditions might not be covered in 2019—which can be a real problem if your pet develops a chronic condition.

- **Read your policy carefully and ask questions:** Most policies require deductibles, co-pays or both. Look for coverage with simple, percentage-based payouts and no reliance on judgments of what's "reasonable." Also check them out for:

    - **Covered conditions:** Some pet insurance policies may reimburse covered medical expenses for accidents, illnesses, surgeries, X-rays, prescriptions, hospitalizations, emergencies or cancer treatments. Other plans may only cover accident and illness after a waiting period.

    - **Pre-existing conditions:** Insurers consider hereditary and certain medical conditions as pre-existing conditions.

    - **Exclusions:** Treatments not covered by pet insurance can vary by type of pet or breed.

- **Catastrophic coverage:** If you plan to use the insurance for catastrophic coverage—say, $1,000 and up—go for the highest deductible you can comfortably afford.

- **Cheaper by the dozen?** Does the insurer give a discount for insuring multiple pets?

Did You Know?

Many dog owners are having a harder time getting homeowner's liability insurance if they have a certain breed of dog. Or they are paying higher premiums if they have dogs who are considered to be one of the more dangerous breeds.

If you are planning to buy a home or switch policies, read the fine print for exclusions that may include your breed. Some breeds that have been listed include:

- Akita
- Bull mastiffs
- Chows
- Doberman pinschers
- German shepherds
- Huskies
- Pit bull terriers
- Rottweillers
- Staffordshire terriers
- Wolf-dog hybrids

Doggy Drugs for Less

Looking for a way to save some money on your dog's medications?

Maricopa County offers a prescription drug–card program that gives a break on both human and pet medications. It was one of the first in the country to offer discounts for both. The card is free and offers an average savings of 20 percent on prescription drugs.

All county residents, regardless of age, income or existing health coverage, may use the card. However, it can't be used with any other prescription drug program.

The card is accepted at more than 80 percent of the pharmacies in the Valley. The only pet medications that are covered are ones that are also used by humans—for example, human insulin used to treat diabetic cats. There are no restrictions or limits on frequency of use.

After the county began its program, the city of Mesa followed suit and offers a similar program to its residents and their pets. As does AAA.

You can also try getting your pet's prescription filled at regular drugstores so long as that same drug is also prescribed to humans. Walgreens allows customers to enroll pets as family members and take advantage of its prescription-savings club. Costco can be a great option for prescriptions and you don't have to be a member to get medications there.

Another choice is to shop at one of the Veterinary-Verified Internet Pharmacy Practice Sites accredited by the National Association of Boards of Pharmacy.

Did You Know?

Metro Phoenix is home to the Midwestern University College of Veterinary Medicine, which educates veterinarians and operates a teaching hospital that provides high-quality veterinary care accessible to the general public.

Midwestern's Companion Animal Clinic offers a wide range of veterinary services, including wellness and primary care, internal medicine, surgery, neurology, oncology, dental care, CT scans, rehabilitation therapy and even hemodialysis. Many dog patients are referred to the clinic for specialty care by their family veterinarians. At the clinic, they will be seen by both student veterinarians-in-training and faculty members who are licensed veterinarians.

Veterinary teaching hospitals can provide several benefits for their patients: enthusiastic students are terrific patient advocates, the medicine practiced is based on the latest advances and the faculty all have advanced training. "The Companion Animal Clinic is an excellent option for those who are looking for affordable, state-of-the-art care and want to support the education of future veterinarians in Arizona," says Dr. Jason Eberhardt, the clinic's director. The only drawback, he says, is that "learning takes time and appointments will be longer than with your family veterinarian."

There is a perception among consumers that veterinary teaching hospitals' charges are lower than other facilities, but schools say that's not true. Midwestern officials say the Companion Animal Clinic has a uniquely affordable pricing structure.

Your Dog's Sex Life

The easiest way to reduce the suffering of animals is to reduce the number of unwanted animals.

Through Fix.Adopt.Save, a coalition of six metro Phoenix animal-welfare organizations, our community continues to focus on spay/neuter programs. Over the past four years, these surgeries have increased by 12 percent, resulting in a 42 percent decrease in intake at area shelters.

Spaying or neutering your dog can help you as well as the animal community. Here are five good reasons to spay or neuter your dog:

- **Better health:** You can actually prolong your dog's life by spaying or neutering because the procedures eliminate the chances of uterine or testicular cancer and, in females, spaying dramatically cuts the chance of breast cancer. Also, you reduce your chances of facing hundreds of dollars in vet bills.

- **Better behavior (male):** A male dog who is neutered when young is much less likely to mark his territory or get into fights with other male dogs. He won't break through the fence to get to a female in heat. And he's also less likely to bite someone.

- **Easier care (female):** Maybe you like the idea of putting doggy diapers on your dog twice a year for 10 days straight to protect your house while she is in heat. Then again, maybe not.

- **Cheaper licenses:** In Maricopa County, there's a price break on licenses for altered dogs.

- **Keeping your friends:** There are only so many times you can ask them to take one of your new puppies. Chances are you are going to run out of friends before you run out of puppies.

The Valley has a number of low-cost or free spay/neuter programs:

- **Animal Defense League of Arizona:** Perhaps your first call should be to their Spay/Neuter Hotline at 1-866-952-SPAY (toll-free) for referrals to low-cost spay/neuter programs closest to you.

- **Altered Tails:** The largest nonprofit spay/neuter organization in Arizona has sterilized more than 100,000 dogs and cats since its inception. Phone: (602) 943-7729.

- **Arizona Humane Society:** The AHS has two clinics that offer low-cost spaying and neutering. One is in south Phoenix and the other is in the Sunnyslope area of north Phoenix. South Phoenix phone: (602) 997-7586; Sunnyslope phone: (602) 997-7585.

When Disaster Strikes

Would you know what to do if an emergency big or small hit your house? And, just as importantly, how could you help your dog in such a situation?

It's true that Phoenix doesn't get hurricanes or tornadoes but we do get a lot of heat. And those boiling hot summertime temperatures can cause power outages or air-conditioning breakdowns that can be disastrous if not handled right.

And we do get our share of flash floods, especially in more undeveloped areas of the Phoenix metro area.

To be prepared for any type of emergency, emergency-management specialists recommend keeping a "bug-out" bag ready for each family member, including the four-legged ones.

A typical canine bug-out bag can include:

- Veterinarian records
- Food (can opener if necessary)
- Water
- Medicine
- Leashes and collars
- Bedding
- Toys

It's also a good idea to put stickers on your pet's carrier with your name and phone number. Include a phone number for someone like a relative or neighbor who has agreed to care for your pet in case of an emergency.

Veterinarian records are critical because if your dog must go to an emergency shelter you want to make sure the shelter knows if he has any special health needs. Many emergency shelters, including those run by the American Red Cross, won't accept animals. Having your dog's vaccination records may be helpful if you can find a shelter willing to take dogs.

Malinda Malone, who teaches pet safety courses in Ahwatukee, also says people should have photos of their dog stashed in several different places: cell phones, safety deposit boxes, with out-of-state relatives. The photos can really help in finding and confirming your dog's identity if you are separated.

The American Veterinary Medical Association and the American Red Cross also offer these suggestions:

- **Give me shelter:** Have a list of pet-friendly hotels and motels, including phone numbers. If you have notice of an impending disaster, call ahead for reservations.

- **Give my dog shelter:** Have a list of boarding facilities and veterinarians who could shelter your pets in an emergency.

- **Be secure:** In case of an emergency, keep your dog on a secure leash if you are out of the house or in the car.

- **Be aware:** In stressful situations, even the most trustworthy pets may panic, hide, try to escape, bite or scratch.

Unexpected Heatwaves

It gets hot, hot, hot here in the summer. Back East, they have snow days, which means is people stay at home to escape the cold and the chaos. In Arizona, our version of snow days is AC days. If your home's AC is broken or your car's AC konks out, there's a general understanding that dealing with the AC takes precedence and everything else (work, school, social life) is put on the back burner.

What happens to you and the dog if your air-conditioning goes kaput? What if there is a power blackout?

Well, the short answer is that you sweat a lot and the dog pants a lot and you start looking for solutions *muy pronto*:

- **Time to fire up an emergency generator:** Many of them use natural gas as a source of fuel and are installed outdoors in a secure cabinet.

- **Fans:** Battery-powered fans can get the air moving

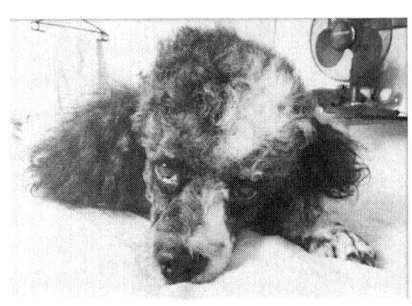

- **Cool down:** Bathing your dog or cat in cool water or wrapping them in wet towels can help to reduce their body temperature.

- **Access to water:** Put out an extra water bowl or two to make sure your dog is drinking. Especially important for senior dogs who overheat more easily. Or those with shorter noses like bulldogs, boxers, Shih Tzus.

- **Recognize heatstroke signs:** They include glazed eyes, excessive drooling, a rapid heart rate, dizziness or lack of coordination, fever, lethargy and loss of consciousness, according to the American Humane Society.

- **Make some calls:** It's time to ask for help and get you and the dog to a friend's cooler house. When all else fails, Google pet-friendly hotels and get to one.

In Case of Fire

How do you protect your dog if there is a fire in the house?

Being prepared will help make sure all your loved ones, including the four-legged ones, survive.

First, check the batteries in your smoke detectors. Perhaps do it every year on your birthday. Make sure the smoke detectors are working—then you can load up on all those birthday candles.

Get the Info Out There

Rural/Metro Fire Department suggests displaying stickers in your home's front window that allow you to list the number of pets in your home. Stickers are available at pet-supply stores or from the American Society for the Prevention of Cruelty to Animals. Consider getting the static cling version so you can easily remove them for updates.

The Best Friends Dog Club of Sun City has its own sticker solution. Instead of using a sticker, they fill out a form and put it inside a pill bottle that is placed inside their refrigerator's butter dish area. The fire department knows to check the fridge in case of fire.

In addition to letting people know how many pets are at your house, it is also a good idea to know where a leash is at all times. If you have to leave the house in a hurry, having your dog on a leash can help reduce the confusion.

Fire departments like Rural/Metro are increasingly better equipped to rescue pets at risk. Their units now have "Fido bags," oxygen masks specially made for dogs and cats. A local nonprofit, the Fetch Foundation, has donated Fido bags to Valley fire department.

Saying Goodbye

Dogs—their only true fault is they usually die before we do.

And people who love dogs are frequently faced with the heartbreaking task of deciding when is it time to help our best friends die. It is such a difficult decision, but there are resources that can help you during this very stressful time.

How Do You Know When It Is Time?

Most likely, you have developed a very close relationship with your veterinarian as you have worked together over the years to keep your dog healthy. Now, during this time of illness, your bond with the veterinarian and their staff has probably only deepened. Ask the vet and the staff for their guidance. Many vets will tell you that in evaluating how the dog is doing you should consider how they are eating, drinking, peeing, pooping and loving life. And many vets will say in the gentlest of ways that when it comes to putting a dog to sleep, it is better to be a day or a week too early rather than to be a day too late.

Most times, this important decision doesn't have to be made immediately in the vet's office. You will have a chance to talk it over with your family, friends and others who know you and the dog. Their counsel can be helpful but ultimately it is your decision on what is best for your dog.

In addition to your veterinarian, there are now pet hospice services that provide at-home care for your animal, including urgent-care services and medications that can help with your dog's discomfort, as well as in-home euthanasia. Keeping your very ill dog at home as much as possible can help you and the dog during these difficult last days.

Help for Grieving Humans

Hospice of the Valley offers a pet-loss support group the first Saturday of every month and has done so for 20 years now, says Mara Goebel, group leader. Hospice of the Valley is the leading nonprofit hospice provider (for humans) in metro Phoenix.

Goebel got involved in the group as a participant after her beloved 17-year-old poodle died. Goebel healed better after talking with others about her grief, and she realized the critical importance of providing a place where people could honestly express their feelings of loss after the death of their faithful companions.

"In the group no one rolls their eyes or tells you that it was just a dog," Goebel says. "They don't tell you just to get a new one. Would people say that if someone's husband died? Just get a new one?"

Every month, a dozen or more people come to the group looking for a safe, steady source of support. Some people's animals have just died; others are grieving pets who died years ago.

The group also sees people who are returning after losing another pet. "They know they can come back here and we will be available to them," Goebel says. "It's a great source of comfort knowing that someone is here who cares."

What to Say to Someone Who Has Lost Their Dog

As a dog lover, you will likely feel a great deal of sympathy toward someone who has just lost their dog. But how do you express that sympathy in a helpful way?

Say little and listen a lot, says Mara Goebel, who leads a pet-loss support group for Hospice of the Valley. Just begin the conversation by saying that you are so sorry to hear the news and tell them that you are there for them. Be prepared to listen as long as needed. It's crucial for people who are in pain to express themselves. Grief-induced isolation and silence only thwarts healing, Goebel says.

Avoid saying "I know how you feel" even though you are feeling empathy toward your friend.

Individuals grieve differently. Some feel that they didn't do enough for their dog; others feel guilty that they are grieving more for their dog than a deceased human relative. Some want to fill the void in their hearts immediately and get another dog; others can't even think of the possibility of having another animal in the house.

"There is no right way or wrong way. Everyone does it differently," Goebel says. "Just be patient with them as they go through this."

Your Dog and the Law

Illegal Beagles and Other Dog-Law FAQs

For such seemingly carefree creatures, dogs invite a lot of lawmaking. In fact, the State Bar of Arizona has its own animal-law section, an up-and-coming area of law that deals with everything from animal-cruelty cases to estate planning for companion pets. It was one of the first legal associations in the country to zero in on animal-related legal quandaries.

Also, it seems like every year new legislation is proposed at the state legislature or in city halls regarding dogs and other companion pets. Perhaps it is an indication of how important pets are to Arizonans. Here are some of the most common canine-related legal questions/concerns for people who live in the metro Phoenix area:

City or county: Who does what when it comes to my dog?

For most of us who live in urban Maricopa County, there are two different authorities over our little dog friends: the county and the city/town where we live.

Maricopa County Animal Care and Control enforces leash laws, pet licensing and animal bite issues. The rest—dog barking, wayward pooping, number of dogs in a home—fall under the city and town you live in, if there are rules at all.

Illegal Beagles and Other Dog-Law FAQs

Does my dog have to be licensed?

All dogs must be vaccinated for rabies and have a current Maricopa County dog license. For information on how to vaccinate and license your dog, please call (602) 506-PETS (7387).

It pays to have your dog licensed. Dogs who bite someone and who do not have a current Maricopa County dog license or a current rabies vaccination are usually quarantined at a county shelter or at a veterinarian's office. If your dog is vaccinated and licensed and the bite is considered "non-severe," you may be able to keep him under quarantine in your home.

Why do I need to have my dog licensed?

Uh…it's the law. Arizona law requires that all dogs three months of age and older must be vaccinated against rabies and licensed. Maricopa County Animal Care and Control handles this for all municipalities within the county (with the exception of Fountain Hills and Native American reservations).

Dog owners must complete a license application within 15 days of vaccination. Residents new to Maricopa County and new dog owners must purchase a license within 30 days. A penalty will be assessed to owners who do not apply within the required time line. Failure to license a dog is a Class 2 misdemeanor.

My neighbor's dogs are always barking. What can I do about it?

Barking dogs is one of the city of Phoenix's hot-button topics. Interestingly enough, calls about barking dogs tend to go down in the summer months—people have their homes shut up tight because of the heat and sound is less likely to travel. Come nice weather, complaints about barking dogs increase.

Most cities and towns in the area have laws against barking dogs and all municipalities encourage neighbors to work the issue between themselves. Their suggestions include:

- ❧ Try to talk to your neighbor when you are not frustrated about the barking.

- ❧ When you approach your neighbor, be calm and plan to discuss the barking in a friendly manner.

- ❧ Inform them of the time of day or night that the dog is barking.

- ❧ Ask the neighbor whether you can contact them, day or night, when the barking is a problem.

- ❧ If leaving a note for your neighbor:
  - Explain what the dog does when the family is away from home.
  - Choose words that are not offensive or intimidating to the dog owner.
  - If you feel safe doing so, leave them your name, telephone number, or address so they can respond to your letter.

If the barking doesn't stop, perhaps it is time for mediation. The city of Phoenix reports that its mediation program with a trained neutral mediator has been very effective when it comes to settling neighbor vs. neighbor dog disputes.

If mediation doesn't work, it is time to document the situation because you may be going to court. The city of Phoenix requires that at least three parties sign a barking-dog complaint. If you can't get the signatures, you must submit at least a video, audio or a written log of the barking dog. Once the submission is accepted, you will have to appear before a judge to sign the complaint and then agree to appear and testify at a trial.

In the city of Phoenix, a violation of the Barking Dog Ordinance is a Class 1 misdemeanor, and a person found responsible can be fined up to $2,500.

Can I bring my dog into restaurants?

Many restaurants will let you have your dog with you on the patio. And all restaurants are required to allow service dogs into the indoor portion of the restaurant.

The rub, legally speaking, is when you try to pass off your dog as a service animal and he isn't. Under a state law passed in 2018, it is illegal for a pet owner to "fraudulently misrepresent an animal as a service animal" to business owners. People who break the law could be fined $250.

Do I have to have my dog on a leash all the time?

Arizona really tries to discourage free-range dogs. State laws say that a dog should be enclosed on an owner's property or on a leash not to exceed six feet in length, directly under the owner's control.

Recently, there has been discussion about what is allowed if you are at a deserted park—is it OK to let your dog run free? Under Phoenix municipal code, the leash law doesn't have to be followed if you are in an area designated as a dog park.

I heard tethering a dog is against the law?

Tempe, Phoenix and Glendale have anti-tethering laws for dogs. They ban people from leaving their dogs tied up outside without supervision or when it is hotter than 85 degrees outside.

The laws were passed to protect dogs but also neighbors, because tied dogs can bark loudly and become aggressive.

The maximum fine for violating the law is $500, but offenders can reduce that if they agree to community service or a diversion program.

What do I do if I think an animal is being mistreated?

If you witness an animal being beaten, attacked or harmed in any way, immediately call 911.

Anyone with information about a felony animal abuse case anywhere in Maricopa County can call Silent Witness at (480) WITNESS. You can also call the Maricopa County Sheriff's Office

Investigations Unit at (602) 876-TIPS (8477) or email the unit at tips@mcso.maricopa.gov.

You can also call your local police department or the Arizona Humane Society Ambulance Service/Cruelty Investigations at (602) 997-7585 ext. 2073.

What happens to someone who is reported for hoarding dogs?

Under the city of Phoenix laws, individuals can face a Class 1 misdemeanor if they are convicted of having 10 or more animals under circumstances "injurious" to the health or welfare of any animal or person.

People who are found guilty of hoarding must also undergo a mental-health evaluations.

Can I break a car window if I see a dog trapped in the car?

Recognizing how dangerous it can be for dogs to be trapped in hot cars, the state of Arizona recently passed a "good Samaritan" law that allows people to take drastic, window-smashing measures without fear of being sued later over broken windows. The new law also covers children who are trapped in cars.

Breaking a window is legal as long as you meet three criteria:

- 🐾 You must notify law enforcement or emergency personnel first.
- 🐾 You must in good faith believe the child's or pet's life is in danger.
- 🐾 You must remain with the child or pet until emergency personnel arrive.

Is it illegal to get a dog from a pet store?

Reacting to anti–puppy mill laws passed by certain Arizona cities, the state recently approved a new law that requires

Arizona pet stores to purchase puppies from U.S. Department of Agriculture (USDA) licensed breeders.

USDA requires any breeder that has more than four female breeding dogs to be licensed. If a breeder has less than four female dogs, they don't need a license and can still sell to Arizona pet stores. If a pet store is caught three times buying from an unlicensed breeder, the store will be required to only buy dogs from shelters and rescue groups.

Laws passed by Phoenix and Tempe offer greater protection against the sale of puppy mill dogs, and animal-rights groups argue that the state law is a weaker version of the cities' regulations. They also point out that federal regulation is not strong enough to make sure the puppies bought from national breeders are being treated humanely.

Can a landlord refuse to rent to me because I have a dog?

Yes, a landlord or a commercial management company can refuse to rent to you if you have a dog. The only exception comes when you have a service dog. The federal Fair Housing Act requires that landlords make "reasonable accommodations" for tenants with disabilities. Allowing a service dog can be such an accommodation. And that includes emotional-support dogs as well.

If you do have a service dog and the dog damages the property (which is unlikely because they are usually so well trained), you will be liable for any damages.

> **Did You Know?**
> Only eight states require veterinarians to report suspected cases of animal abuse. Those states are Arizona, California, Colorado, Illinois, Minnesota, Nebraska, Oklahoma and West Virginia.

Cracking Down on Vicious Dogs

Arizona now has tougher penalties for owners of aggressive and vicious dogs because of a Glendale couple's determination that no other dog should die as theirs did.

Fabian's Law (aka "Vicious Dog Owner Responsibility Act") has strong penalties for those who allow their dogs to attack humans or other dogs.

The law was a labor of love for Richard and Sally Andrade, who in 2009 saw their beloved miniature apricot poodle, Fabian, fatally attacked. Sally was walking Fabian on a leash one evening when a pit bull charged them. Sally worked desperately to free Fabian from the pit bull's vise-like mouth and rushed her beloved dog to an emergency animal hospital, but it was too late.

The Glendale couple pushed for state legislation after learning they couldn't hold the other dog's owner accountable for Fabian's death.

In the same year that Fabian was killed, there were 580 "dog-on-dog" attacks in Maricopa County.

Now, because of the Andrades' hard work, Arizona has a state law against dog-on-dog attacks and tougher penalties for owners of aggressive and vicious dogs, including dogs who are licensed, who attack other dogs and humans.

Under Fabian's Law, an owner who fails to control their vicious dog and prevent attacks on people can be charged with a felony instead of a misdemeanor. It's a Class 3 felony that carries a jail sentence of more than three years. There are exceptions for cases of self-defense and protection of others.

Penalties can go as high as a Class 5 felony for having a dog who has a history of biting or who has been found to be a vicious animal.

It's now a Class 1 misdemeanor if the owner fails to keep their vicious dog from escaping their home. A Class 1 misdemeanor can bring six months in jail.

The new laws also make a distinction between vicious and aggressive dogs.

In their drive to change state law, the Andrades were helped by hundreds of neighbors and animals lovers as well as dog groomers and Maricopa County Animal Care and Control.

The Andrades now run a nonprofit that helps people and animals who are victims of vicious dog attacks. Sally Andrade is clear that her group isn't against certain dog breeds. "We just want to make sure dog owners are responsible for their dogs."

Fabian's death by a vicious dog began an effort in Arizona to make dog owners more responsible. Photo courtesy of fabianslaw.org

When Fido Turns on You

Welcome to metro Phoenix, one of the Dog Bite Capitals of the country.

Just ask your friendly neighborhood mail carrier. Over the past three years, metro Phoenix has moved up the rankings of cities where dogs attack postal carriers. One of the reasons for our high ranking is that we have a large number of loose dogs, and the U.S. Postal Service is trying to reduce the number of dog problems faced by carriers.

If you want to keep on the good side of your mail carrier, just alert the post office via your online package pickup application that there is a dog at your home. That information makes it into the scanners they use as they make deliveries. The scanners also keep them posted on other dog-related information, such as an animal running off-leash. Another good idea is to secure your dog in a separate room if you know that you have packages being delivered; some dogs have crashed through plate-glass doors and windows just to get at a mail carrier.

It pays to play nice with the mail carrier. If a mail carrier feels threatened by your dog, they can stop delivery and have you come to the post office for your mail.

It's not just mail carriers either: The Arizona Department of Health Services says that severe dog bites requiring overnight hospital stays have more than doubled over the last five years. More than 70 percent of the injuries happened in homes.

Recognizing Dangerous Dogs

Hard to believe, but even your little couch potato can become a dangerous dog. If he is ill or feels threatened, he can snap (literally, snap at you). The American Medical Veterinary Association says that just because you've had a positive interaction with a dog before doesn't mean it's guaranteed to happen that way again. Remain alert to risks from dogs, even those you think you know.

The association also recommends that when meeting a dog, offer the back of your hand and see whether the dog is comfortable approaching and sniffing. Interactions initiated by the dog are safer because the dog is coming to you and wants to interact. To be safe, ask the person on the other end of the leash about meeting the dog. Another bit of great advice from the association: sometimes, people are reluctant to admit that their dog can become aggressive. So, if you ask someone if their dog wants to meet you or your dog and that person is ambivalent, just take the hint and move on.

Some people will tie a yellow ribbon or orange bandana around their dog's leash as a warning that the dog may become aggressive. The yellow means "proceed with caution" and can also indicate a dog is fearful, prone to overexcitement or just not good with children.

How Can I Avoid Getting Bitten?

The Arizona Animal Welfare League has a few tips for dealing with aggressive dogs:

- **Stand like a tree:** Ignore the dog completely. Don't smile or show your teeth—those are signs of aggression to a dog.

- **If the dog attacks:** If the dog bites you, go to the ground, crawl up in a little ball, cover your ears and head and wait. Most likely it will leave you alone. Anything moving is like prey to the dog.

- **Be calm:** Don't try to outrun a dog or escape it by bike; it's not a good idea. Don't yell or scream either. And don't try to break up a dog fight by yourself.

- **Don't assume:** Many times people will become fearful only around certain breeds, forgetting that any dogs can attack if they feel threatened or unwell.

- **Be alert:** Never go near a dog who has newborn puppies, or is near food, or is on a chain outside or inside a car. Dogs will try to protect their area.

The Arizona Animal Welfare League has classes on how to train a dog to be less aggressive.

A Dog Bit Me. What Do I Do?

First, get medical care. Dogs' mouths are repositories of bacteria and their bites can lead to infection. You may need antibiotics, particularly if you have gotten a deep puncture wound. Also, any unidentified dog runs the risk of carrying rabies. So, if the dog cannot be identified or if the owner cannot show proof of rabies vaccination, seek medical attention immediately.

Then call (602) 506-PETS (7387) to complete a bite report.

Dogs as Heroes

College Dogs

Is your dog smart? Like, college smart?

Perhaps there is a place for him at Arizona State University.

ASU is home to the Canine Science Collaboratory, a part of the university's psychology department focused on looking at the behavior of dogs, especially when it comes to human interactions.

Led by behavioral scientist Clive Wynne, the collaboratory has conducted academic research on a wide-ranging field of topics such as the effect of labeling dogs by breeds in shelters (can be detrimental) to the exact age when puppies are their cutest to humans (it's eight weeks).

Academic interest in dog behavior dates back to Ivan Pavlov (ring a bell?), a Russian physiologist who noticed that his dogs, after being fed by him frequently and regularly, began to salivate whenever he walked into a room—whether he had the feed bag or not. His work involving "conditioned response" (dog getting hungry just by seeing the food provider) helped create new fields in psychology.

A lot of that early work was forgotten until a resurgence of interest at the very end of the last century, Wynne says.

Why Look at Dog-Human Relationships

Hundreds of millions of people share their homes with dogs. Most of the time this is a happy coexistence, but things can go wrong too, Wynne says. Dogs can suffer from separation anxiety and other psychological disorders; people can get bitten and harmed in other ways.

Why not get reliable scientific information about how best to live together in harmony?, he asks.

The collaboratory's work goes beyond looking at the dog who is hanging out on the family room sofa. By better understanding dogs who end up in shelters, we can reduce the number of dogs who must be euthanized because of lack of space or who end up staying in the kennel much longer than is good for them, Wynne says.

"We have committed to many research projects looking to better understand how to reduce stress for dogs living in shelters and help them find lasting homes," Wynne said.

How You Can Help with Research

The collaboratory's studies are focused on better understanding the behavior of dogs and their cognitive abilities. They typically involve the dogs learning silly games and getting snacks for playing them, says Lisa Gunter, a doctoral candidate who studies at the collaboratory. Gunter has published academic papers on behavior in shelter dogs.

There's little risk to participating and it's a wonderful opportunity for learning and enrichment.

The team works with dogs of all breeds and ages (except for young dogs—under six months of age—or those that are newly owned).

Ongoing studies include investigating the effect of aging on cognition in memory tasks and looking at factors that influence the rate at which dogs learn to detect different odors. The collaboratory is particularly interested in modernizing the techniques used to train odor detection "sniffer" dogs.

Dogs on Duty

Around 5:30 p.m. on one Saturday in 2005, Phoenix police officer Bryan Hanania and his police dog, R. J., responded to a call of theft and carjacking in central Phoenix. The suspect had ditched the car and was trying to get away on foot. R. J., a three-year-old Belgian Malinois—and one of 18 highly trained Phoenix police dogs—tracked him.

The Malinois ran after him and, after coming face-to-face with R. J., the suspect got back into his car. Then the suspect turned the car around and aimed it for Hanania and R. J. He struck R. J., whose spinal cord was crushed, and R. J. was euthanized that evening.

R. J. had been with Officer Hanania and the Phoenix Police Department's canine unit for 18 months and had been used more than 300 times to sniff out narcotics and apprehend suspects.

In 2006, a memorial for canine officers like R. J., who were killed in the line of duty, debuted in the Wesley Bolin Memorial Plaza in downtown Phoenix. The striking memorial features a large bronze of a German shepherd and lists the names of fallen canine officers.

Dogs have long been defenders of hearth and home and the Valley's public safety dogs are no exception.

Several different breeds of dogs are typically used to protect the public: German shepherds and Belgian Malinois as police and military dogs; Australian shepherds for search and rescue; bloodhounds to track down runaway prisoners and Labradors for arson investigation.

Highly Trained

Specially trained police dogs are used to search buildings and specific areas, detect narcotics and explosives, and track and apprehend suspects.

Other trained dogs can sniff out cocaine, marijuana, methamphetamines and heroin.

Bomb-sniffing dogs are trained to detect and alert their handlers to dozens of different odors such as dynamite and C-4, while cadaver dogs can find decaying human tissue, bones and fluids.

Training can go beyond the nose. Phoenix police dogs are physically conditioned to withstand hot weather and they can jump off hovering helicopters. Just as important as the physical training, is the socialization. Police dogs are used in all different types of settings and they need to be calm enough to be around crowds and even curious kids.

More than 300 dogs are part of Arizona police departments. It can be dangerous duty no matter what the assignment. In fact, some dogs are outfitted with two-pound Kevlar vests to protect them against bullet wounds and knife stabs.

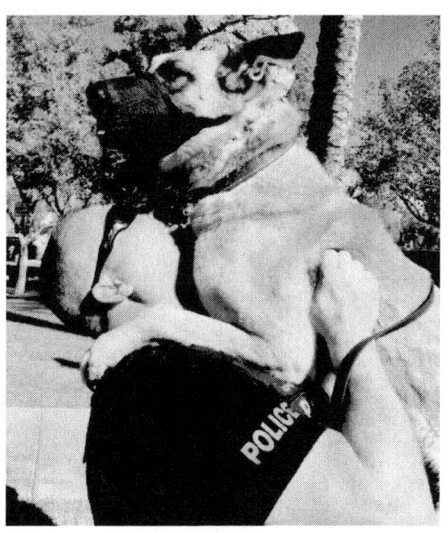

Ado enjoys being a K-9 officer with Glendale Police Department.

Dogs as Healers

For every type of human being who needs help—children, seniors, hospital patients, people with a disability or those facing death—there is a therapy (or service) dog to help.

Health care providers recognize that dogs (and other animals) offer just the right kind of medicine for people in need. Pet therapy visits have been shown to relieve stress, lower blood pressure and even improve self-esteem.

There are a number of places throughout metro Phoenix where you and your four-legged cure-all can be put to good use—here is just a sampling:

For Kids

- 🐾 **Gabriel's Angels:** Gabriel's Angels delivers pet therapy to abused, neglected and at-risk children. The nonprofit helps 14,600 at-risk kids by visiting crisis nurseries, homeless and domestic violence shelters and schools.

- 🐾 **Paws to Read:** The city of Glendale and Paws to Read have joined forces to

let students practice reading aloud to a certified therapy dog like the wonderfully friendly Sammy. Children who may feel uncomfortable with their reading skills get to practice in front of an always-appreciative listener.

For Adults

- **The Companion Animal Association of Arizona, Inc.** has operated in the Phoenix metro area since 1986. They visit thousands of elderly, sick and disabled people in hospitals, nursing homes and other care facilities.

    The group got its start in an interesting way. In 1982, a statewide task force with the support of 30 state, federal, and community agencies met to hold the first Arizona Conference on Companion Animals for the elderly. The task force created the Companion Animal Association of Arizona, Inc. One of its first new jobs was to make sure that new state laws were being followed and that the elderly and people with disabilities were able to keep their companion pets in public housing.

For Hospital Patients

- Chances are that every major hospital near you has a pet therapy program. Each hospital will differ when it comes to requirements of what kind of training you and your dog will have to go through before being able to make hospital rounds.

For Terminally Ill Patients

- **Hospice of the Valley:** Its Pet Connections program makes visits to many different settings: inpatient hospice homes, skilled nursing facilities, group homes and patients' private homes.

> **Did You Know?**
>
> Therapy dogs are not the same as service or assistance dogs. Service dogs are specially trained to directly assist humans, and have a legal right to accompany their owners in most areas. They are not considered "pets."
>
> Service dogs are legally protected by the Americans with Disabilities Act of 1990.
>
> Therapy dogs do not provide direct assistance and are not mentioned in the Americans with Disabilities Act. If the sign says "No Dogs Allowed," that includes them.

Your Dog and Therapy

Could your dog help people in trouble with a wag of his tail or a smile on his face?

Any breed or size of dog can become a therapy dog as long as he has one important thing: an excellent temperament.

He also must really like human contact because in his prospective line of work, he is going to be held, stroked and squeezed in sometimes really clumsy ways. Sometimes a wheelchair may even inadvertently roll over his tail.

Before evaluating your dog, make sure you as his handler want to take this on. Therapy Dog International recommends asking these questions of yourself:

- 🐾 Do I enjoy visiting health care/educational facilities?
- 🐾 Do I enjoy meeting strangers and making conversation with them?
- 🐾 Am I comfortable interacting with children and/or the elderly, people in hospitals or people with disabilities?
- 🐾 Do I have the time to make this type of commitment?

Now it's time to evaluate your dog.

- **Is your dog healthy** and at least one year old?

- **How does your dog react to strangers?** A good prospect for therapy work will enjoy meeting people. He will actively—but calmly—approach them. A dog who is so happy he jumps up or pushes with feet, body or nose, will need some training. A dog who is fearful or aggressive should not be considered for therapy work.

- **How does your dog react to unusual events?** What happens when an alarm clock rings, the smoke alarm goes off or a book falls off a shelf? Your dog should show interest in these unexpected events, but should be calm. If your dog barks at a knock on the door, he should be quiet and under control when you open the door.

- **Does your dog have basic good manners?** Will he sit and lie down when you tell him to? How is your dog around other dogs?

- **What is your dog's true personality?** Your dog must be willing to put up with accidental and intentional pain that may be inflicted, such as clumsy petting or a wheelchair rolling over a paw or tail.

If you still think your dog has what it takes, then it's time to take him in for basic obedience training. After obedience training, your dog must be certified. Therapy Dogs International, Therapy Dogs Inc. and Delta Society are three well-recognized organizations that register dogs. Contact the therapy group that you are interested in volunteering with and they will let you know which credentialing organization they prefer.

How You Can Help

You just love your dog. In fact, you pretty much like every dog you meet. And someday after looking at all those big Hershey-colored eyes, wagging tails and goofy and serious expressions, you're struck by the idea of helping out dogs. It's almost as if these big-hearted creatures inspire us to try to be a-little-bit-better people.

You know the saying "Help me be the kind of person my dog thinks I am"? Well, helping out dogs and other animals may be a great place to begin your personal self-improvement plan.

But where exactly to start?

Turns out, just as there is a wide range of dogs, there is a wide range of opportunities to help our four-legged friends.

Your Time

Volunteer reading to dog. Photo courtesy Arizona Animal Welfare League

You would volunteer at a shelter but you would end up taking all the animals home—at least that is the worry that stops you from volunteering. But, actually, mass adoption by bighearted volunteers doesn't happen that often, says Michael Morefield of Arizona Animal Welfare League. Instead, volunteers become genuinely excited about bringing a dog together with a new family, he says. In his three years at AAWL, for example, Moorefield has brought home only one dog from the shelter. "Bratty Addie" was returned four times to AAWL for her shyness; Morefield just decided it was destiny that she come home with him and be one of his dogs.

If you still aren't sure of your willpower, consider volunteering in a way that reduces your exposure to adoptable animals. From laundry to cleaning to office work, a lot of ways to help at a rescue/shelter don't involve hands-on-animals experience.

Or you can volunteer in a way that limits your time with them. Shelters and rescues always need photos taken of their animals to make it easier for them to be adopted. You can go in, snap some photos and help load them to a website. A quick, easy way to make a huge difference in an animal's life!

Or you can do something really fun and volunteer for the Maricopa County Wag and Walk program, which gets shelter dogs out on the county hiking trails and possibly on to a good home with a hiker or someone who likes to walk.

Maricopa County Wag and Walk program. Photo courtesy hikingblogspot.com

Your Stuff

Every animal rescue/shelter has a "wish list" of gear they need, from new turf for a play area to a treadmill that provides summertime exercise to a washing machine. Check to see what is on your favorite rescue's wish list—perhaps it is the very item that is just collecting dust in your garage.

Some items seem to have universal appeal, including sheets, towels and blankets (pillows aren't as preferred—it's not easy to wash them), laundry detergent and wet dog food for hiding pills. Good ol' indestructible Kongs are also always appreciated.

Speaking of stuff, when you feel like buying more stuff, just remember that a number of animal resources also run thrift shops to enhance their budgets. Shopping there can be a good way to support the cause.

Your Money

If you want to help, but don't have the time to volunteer, you can donate money, which is always welcome. Donations can be given once or regularly, such as every month. They also can be made in someone else's name as a gift or in their memory.

Check out who you want to donate to by going to Charity Navigator or the Better Business Bureau's Wise Giving Alliance, which examine charities' finances and operations.

A good rule of thumb is for a charity to spend at least 75 percent of their funds on programs and services.

If you want to be a super-sleuth, check a charity's IRS Form 990, which most nonprofits are required to make public. Guidestar has a searchable database of them. Or simply call the organization and talk with its leaders before writing a check.

Your Special Day

Whether it is a birthday, a wedding day or your dog's Gotcha Day, you can commemorate it by raising money for your favorite organization by dedicating part of your gift registry to shelter donations. Facebook fundraisers have made this especially easy.

Your Attention/Vote

It seems like every year the Arizona Legislature takes up new dog issues. Some legislation sounds great—penalties against animal cruelty and neglect, for example. Other ideas seem kinda weird—like trying to prohibit service dogs from coming into restaurants. If you care about dogs, stay informed through organizations like Humane Voters of Arizona, which keep tabs on our state legislators and pending legislation. And since you care about animals, isn't a good idea to find out how your elected officials vote on these types of issues?

What Your New Dog Needs

Congratulations! You have a new dog. The Arizona Animal Welfare League, which has helped thousands of dogs find loving, new homes, gives these pointers on what your new best friend requires for success:

- **Leash and a collar:** Arizona law requires that leashes be six feet or less.
- **Microchip:** Make sure that the microchip has up-to-date information.
- **Food:** Try to keep your new dog on the same diet until he gets settled.
- **Bowl for food**
- **Bowl for water**
- **Bedding**
- **Toys:** An old T-shirt is an ideal tug toy. Bonus: it carries your scent and the dog will associate that scent with something fun.
- **Treats:** Go easy on them; the dog's tummy is in transition.
- **Neutral space:** If there is another dog in the house, try to introduce the two in a neutral setting to avoid first-time territory-tussle issues.

- **Puppy pads:** Use just until housetraining begins.
- **Recommendations for a veterinarian**
- **Dog-proofing in place:**
  - Think about whether you are going to give the dog access to all of the house.
  - Secure any household cleaners or other poisonous agents.
  - Tape any electrical cords to baseboards.
  - Make sure the fence is sturdy and escape-proof.
  - Check for poisonous plants in the backyard.
- **Extra time:** Plan on being around the house so you can be around your new dog closely for the first 24 hours.
  - **Three days:** The time it takes for the dog to start warming up to you
  - **Three weeks:** The time it takes for the dog to feel like he is fitting in
  - **Three months:** The time it takes for the dog to feel like he is at home

About the Author

Jodie Snyder is an award-winning writer and Arizona native. A former reporter for *The Arizona Republic*, her life changed for the better when she adopted Honeybun from Arizona Beagle Rescue. A rookie to the world of dogs, she decided to find out a little bit more about the species that was taking over her house. Artie is now the house beagle.

About the Illustrator

Jeff Jones is a Phoenix-based illustrator whose clients include IBM, American Express and *The New York Times*. A former designer and art director, Jeff also paints, creates mixed-media pieces and hikes whenever he gets the chance.